DISABILITY
RIGHTS AND WRONGS

DISABILITY
RIGHTS AND WRONGS

Ted Harrison

A LION BOOK

Published by
Lion Publishing plc
Sandy Lane West, Oxford, England
ISBN 0 7459 3138 3
Albatross Books Pty Ltd
PO Box 320, Sutherland, NSW 2232, Australia
ISBN 0 7324 1273 0

First edition 1995
10 9 8 7 6 5 4 3 2 1 0

Acknowledgments
Thanks to the following copyright holders for permission to use extracts.
Every effort has been made to trace copyright holders, and we apologize
if there are any inadvertent omissions or errors in the acknowledgements.
From *Parenting Under Pressure: Mothers and fathers with learning difficulties*
    by Tim and Wendy Booth, Open University Press 1994
The account on p141 appeared in *All People*, the journal of
    Church Action on Disability (CHAD), Spring 1993
From *Images of Disability on Television* by Guy Cumberbatch and Ralph Negrine,
    published by Routledge
The extract and the poem 'Do Unto Others' reprinted on pp74–75 and 142
    from *Mustn't Grumble*, edited by Lois Keith, first published by The Women's Press Ltd,
    1994, 34 Great Sutton Street, London EC1V ODX, are used by permission of
    The Women's Press Ltd.
From *Changing Faces* by James Partridge of Changing Faces, Reg. Charity 1011222,
    1 & 2 Junction Mews, London W2 1PN, published by Changing Faces
From *Mental Handicap: Is anything wrong?* by David Potter,
    published by Kingsway Publications Ltd
From *The Politically Correct Phrasebook* by Nigel Rees published by Bloomsbury
Reproduced from *Cerebral Palsy: A Practical Guide* by Marion Stanton, (Optima, 1992)
The extracts from *Be Not Afraid* by Jean Vanier are reproduced with the permission
    of the publishers, Gill & Macmillan, Dublin
From a Parentability exhibition text © Michele Wates
From *Marie* by Gordon Wilson, published by HarperCollins Publishers Ltd

A catalogue record for this book is available
from the British Library

Printed and bound in Great Britain
by Cox & Wyman Ltd, Reading

CONTENTS

1 Disability Pride   7

2 Rights Not Charity   24

3 Image   38

4 The Value of Life   62

5 The Power Deficit   81

6 Mind and Spirit   98

7 The Disability Debate   111

8 A Re-Evaluation   134

  Index   157

1

Disability Pride

Does the phrase 'disability pride' make sense, or is it a contradiction in terms? For centuries disabled people have laboured under the double burden of fear and pity loaded on them by the rest of society, including the Christian churches, and pride in themselves is the last thing they have felt. But are we moving on? What have disabled people and the churches to say to each other?

For four years up until 1995 I was the presenter of the BBC radio programme 'Does He Take Sugar?', the weekly half hour slot on Radio Four devoted to and specializing in issues concerning disability.

For many years disabled people have known what it is like to be ignored when they are the third person in a three-way conversation. The two able-bodied people speak to each other and refer to the third person only in passing. When it is tea time one able-bodied person asks the other, 'Does he take sugar?'

Fifteen years ago when the BBC started its programme looking at issues of particular interest to disabled people the catch phrase 'Does he take sugar?' was such a good one that it became the title of the programme. Fifteen years on many have wondered whether the joke has passed its sell-by date but try as hard as the producer and others can, no better phrase or title for the programme has been arrived at. While things have vastly improved the 'Does he take sugar?' mentality has not been entirely eradicated; until it is the title to the programme will probably remain.

The early 1990s was an exciting time to be involved with the programme as, over that period, disability became a chic political issue.

For me it was a particularly fascinating assignment. I had reached my forties and the middle-aged are usually thought to be set in their ways of thinking. It was therefore very exciting and stimulating to have one's thought processes, prejudices and attitudes comprehensively challenged. Prior to joining the programme team I had direct personal experience of many of the issues, but I had never analyzed those experiences or viewed them in the way that the radical disability lobby would favour.

Indeed during the five years leading up to 1990 when my life depended on regular kidney dialysis, I would never have contemplated referring to myself as 'disabled'. Despite the limitations of the treatment and my physical capabilities, I remained determined never to downgrade my expectations or opt out of a full life. These are attitudes very recognizable to the current disability lobby, but I would not have appreciated their language or their approach. Thus since 1990, if I can refer to my own learning curve, it has been a mountain climb.

Also before 1990 for many years, my professional work as a journalist had involved me in covering an apparently unrelated field of interest, that of religion. I had presented the Radio Four religious news and current affairs programme 'Sunday' for a number of years and had a spell as the BBC Religious Affairs Correspondent.

This book has its roots in both that world of religious affairs, in which I still remain intently interested, and the world of disability. I have drawn on my own experiences plus those of the many people I have met. I have gone beyond the world of political action to ask moral and ethical questions about disability—to me a basic set of questions, but ones which it seems have only infrequently been addressed so far by others. I hope that in examining these questions I have conveyed the many options open to people seeking answers; not, I hope, in any abstract way but keeping my approach firmly planted in the real world. And I also hope that in the end I have come to some challenging conclusions which others will feel are justified.

A new philosophy

People with disabilities have started a process of 'coming out'. No longer content to be marginalized by society or to be seen as 'cap in hand' recipients of care, many disabled people are constructing and preaching a new philosophy of disability. They draw on the experiences of the civil rights movements and talk of disability pride. They refuse to allow themselves to be downtrodden by social attitudes, they refuse the labels handed down to them by the medical profession. They reject the concept of normality. They are proud to be who they are.

To many in society this is radical thinking and, in their attitudes and insights, this new generation of disabled people is many strides ahead of the majority of members of society. Few people, unacquainted with this perspective on the world, have advanced beyond the traditional ways of viewing and dealing with disability. Most attitudes to disability reflect a jumble of social and individual inner fears, expressed in a number of inappropriate ways ranging from distaste and prejudice to exaggerated concern or saccharin-sweet sentimentality.

That is, unless they too are numbered amongst those who have experienced disability firsthand. In Britain 6 million people are in some way disabled. That firsthand experience of disability will have thrown up a new set of emotions and insights, although in the majority of cases these emotions will not have been politicized.

Some people accept disability fatalistically as their lot in life. Others see it as a challenge, a means to personal and spiritual growth. There are those, too, who see a dark purpose behind their sufferings and frustrations. Many older people take it as a new life-experience which comes with aging. Others born with disabilities will have no wider terms of reference; life with a disability is the only life they know.

But though the politicization of disability is still a minority radical perspective, that way of seeing things is becoming increasingly prevalent.

In the same way that the civil rights movements were started and nurtured by Christians, one might suppose that in the vanguard of this new radicalism there would be a strong Christian input. However there are no equivalents of Martin Luther King. The modern disability movement remains firmly political, not theological. Indeed, many members of the radical disability lobby ally themselves with feminist causes, gay rights issues and other subjects at the 'correct' end of the political spectrum.

However it would be wrong to over-simplify and bracket disability politics with left-wing causes. Some of the most influential opinion formers are to be found wearing ties and waistcoats in such highly respectable organizations as the Royal Association for Disability and Rehabilitation (RADAR).

The politicization of the disability movement may not have invaded the popular psyche, but it nevertheless represents mainstream political thinking; it is not just the prerogative of the enthusiasts and zealots. Yet nevertheless it is firmly secular.

In her practical guide dealing with the subject of cerebral palsy, Marion Stanton, herself a mother of a child with cerebral palsy, wrote:

> **Religious leaders in history have justified gross acts of inhumanity towards people with disabilities... Religion has been misused by people in positions of power to justify the segregation and mis-treatment of a section of society who are misunderstood and undervalued.**

Marion Stanton was not specifically targeting leaders of the Christian faith. She pointed out how the ancient Greeks used to kill disabled children at birth. This was the practice, it would appear, not only because these infants threatened to grow up to be an economic burden, but also because their births were viewed as a form of retribution from the gods.

Far nearer home in time and place, this was the commonly held view in Britain only two centuries ago, a view which went largely unchallenged by church leaders. To quote again from Marion Stanton:

> **In the eighteenth century in Britain 'cripples' were considered to be lower class citizens along with beggars, the unemployed and those who had fallen from grace through vice.**
>
> **In the late eighteenth century institutions started to spring up to which people with disabilities could be removed. These were not places of care and treatment but places where those**

considered a burden and an embarrassment could be kept away from ordinary life where their bodily needs would be met without disruption to society.

As recently as fifty to one hundred years ago, compulsory sterilisation of people considered to be mentally handicapped was taking place in the USA on the theory that it was necessary to reduce the number of 'mental defects' being produced in society.

Although in fairness to Christians it should be pointed out that the age of science gave society new justifications for prejudice. Marion Stanton gave this example:

In the eighteenth century there was a fairly successful move in the deaf community to promote communication by signing. However, under the influence of a school of thought inspired by Charles Darwin, which held that 'defectives' were unnatural and every measure should be taken to eradicate disability, attempts were made to ban signing and to stop deaf people from marrying each other in case it led to the human race becoming deaf. This suppression is still having its effect today with a strong debate still carrying on between those professionals who support signing and those who feel that deaf people must learn to speak in order to fit into society. This is even though there is strong evidence that children who are not allowed to sign are less likely to achieve academically, and are more vulnerable to child abuse, because they have had their means of early communication taken away from them. There are many deaf people today who can remember having their hands tied behind their backs in school in an attempt to force them to communicate orally.

From this it can be seen that both those with a traditional Christian perspective and those with the perspective of unadulterated natural selection have in common a concept of normality and the notion that people with disabilities in some way deviate from or violate that notion. More on that later.

My own story

First, however, I will expand on my own background, for it is perhaps relevant to do so. For nearly twenty-five years I have taken a close interest, as a writer and broadcaster, in questions of faith. It occurred to me back in the seventies, when religion was largely sidelined by the media, that sooner or later questions of faith would return to the news spotlight.

In both the sixties and the seventies it was assumed that world events and political movements could generally be understood in terms of social behaviour. Marxism was still a common theory used to explain change. It involved seeing large groups of people operating as social classes, reacting to economic forces. In all theories, both left- and right-wing, economics was seen as the prime motivator. The Thatcherism of the eighties depended on understanding human beings as predictable, self-centred entities operating in a coherent market system. All in all, economics was elevated to the level of a science. From universities to the media, the belief was held that social change could be best understood and forecast by understanding the mechanisms of the market-place and the way in which the means of production operated.

However, as the years went by it became apparent that questions of belief and faith were every bit as important in determining international events as economics. People did not simply act as consuming automatons. People act emotionally, irrationally and spiritually. The words of Jesus that human beings cannot live by bread alone have not been superseded.

Quite unexpectedly, as far as the media and academic gurus were concerned, other events began to take place in the world. There was the rise of Islam, and the growth of all kinds of fundamentalism, Islamic, Hindu, Jewish and Christian. It also emerged that a key role was being played by churches in places where repressive regimes were being challenged. It was the Roman Catholic church which provided the focus of opposition to the Communists in Poland. It was people like Archbishop Desmond Tutu who spoke for the oppressed majority in South Africa and prepared the ground for the overthrow of apartheid and the dawn of democracy.

Through my work in presenting and reporting for the Radio Four programme 'Sunday' and through spending time as the BBC Religious Affairs Correspondent, I found myself at the centre of an exciting area of work.

I travelled the world, and witnessed many sad and alarming events initiated in the name of religion. I was able to observe many intimate moments of individual faith and uplifting spirituality, and also many examples of intolerant talk and religious bigotry. Not everything that came under a religious label was good. What I recognized was that much of it was very powerful.

Then, at the beginning of the 1980s, I developed an illness as a result of an infection picked up in the course of reporting on an earthquake in Algeria. By 1985 I had a new perspective of the world thrust my way. I spent five years on kidney dialysis and, in that time, learned from front-line experience what it is like to be a patient and to be on the receiving end of care.

As I said earlier, I did not number myself with disabled people but the condition was disabling. There were many things I was simply not able to do as a result of the demands of dialysis and the effects of renal failure. My stamina was limited and such tasks as walking up a flight of stairs presented problems. I also found that my strict diet made it very difficult for me to buy food or drink in a normal way and I discovered firsthand in many small niggling ways how society is designed for the able-bodied and makes few allowances for those who are not.

I discovered too how, when I was a kidney patient, people reacted to me differently in certain subtle ways. This was partly a physical thing. Conversations with people when I was dialyzing had to be conducted at two levels. I was sitting or lying—the other person was standing and looking down. Anyone who uses a wheelchair knows what that feels like.

Perhaps I can quote from my own contemporary account, published five years ago, *Living with Kidney Failure*.

The relationship that develops between staff and patients is an unusual one. Everyone gets to know everyone else very well. Friendships develop, but a feeling persists that the staff believe they have an authority. Any undermining of that authority is resented. And yet to my mind it ought to be a relationship of equals. The staff have an area of specialist knowledge and we, as patients, are their clients. It is certainly essential to my well-being that I am in control of my destiny. I remember times when alarms sounded on a machine to indicate a problem and a young nurse would come over and say, 'Who's causing trouble today then?'

Fortunately throughout my time of kidney dialysis I worked, even travelled and made sure that I did not allow myself to become totally self-absorbed with my condition. Yet as I observed I was unusual in being able to live such a life. Again to quote my own contemporary account:

Many kidney patients do not work because employers do not understand kidney failure and assume that all kidney patients are hopeless invalids. I have even heard it quoted that only 13 per cent of all kidney patients are in employment. If this is the case it is a scandal.

Part of the problem, however, must be the image projected by the patients themselves. In order to raise money for kidney research and other kidney charities or to raise awareness of the need for donor organs, patients have to be presented as sick. Over the years many patients develop a pale, yellow complexion and this reinforces the image that kidney patients are in some way different. One feels for a child struck down by kidney failure whose early life is restricted by the treatment and the technology, but an adult will only really be incapacitated by the illness at the acute stage. Once back into the routine of work and family life, he or she can cope with life very well. Yet this is not widely understood and often families can become too protective and employers too wary and the adult patient is not allowed to resume a normal life. The result of this can sometimes be depression, a feeling of hopelessness and a consequent physical decline or indefinite dependence on the system.

One of the consequences of this can be financial anxiety. Without work the patient becomes dependent on the state and benefits are notoriously ungenerous. Almost all renal units have a social worker who will know his or her way through the benefits maze and it might even be worth those in employment to check if they are entitled to the benefits.

One doctor I spoke to referred to the 'professional kidney patient's syndrome'. This occurs to the patient with no other interests but the illness, who becomes obsessed with his or her misfortune in life.

Some patients are pushed into this role by the system and the inability to find work.

I experienced as well the dilemmas of how to react to people's cloying good intentions. I did not like asking for help. I was, probably still am, too proud for that. Yet there were moments when I needed assistance which was offered but which I stubbornly refused. I recall how travelling south from my home, which was then in Orkney, to the hospital on the mainland, where I was to receive my first dialysis treatment, I refused offers of a wheelchair to take me from the plane to the terminal. With great difficulty I made the journey on my own two feet. Later, as a kidney dialysis patient, I felt uneasy particularly when people, through knowing me, felt they would like to raise money for charities connected with kidney failure.

My experience of renal failure also provided me with the opportunity to discover some deeper understanding of the human condition. I would not have wished the experience of illness on myself—yet it was one, in some ways, I am glad I went through for what I learned from it.

If there is one good thing to be said about renal failure it is that there is the hope of recovery. The path to recovery is long and difficult and takes the form of a transplant operation. I took that road and after certain none-too-pleasant experiences had many of my old physical abilities restored.

Given my wide experience as a broadcaster and my direct experience of a disabling condition I was asked in 1990 if I would become involved in the Radio Four programme 'Does He Take Sugar?' In fact at the time of my transplant operation in 1990 I had appeared on the programme as an interviewee describing renal failure and suggesting ways of living with it.

I spent four years with the programme, in the course of which I got to know many of the people involved in the politics of disability. It was for me a time of surprises. I had not until then known about the affinity many disabled people feel for others caught up and involved in civil rights movements. I had not appreciated disability as a political issue. I was also introduced to the idea that disability was not simply a question of medical classification but involved a re-evaluation of cultural and social attitudes. I became aware of the role of fear and myth in forming prejudice and came to see clearly what is meant when disabled people talk about prejudice.

For the first time I also became aware of the key distinction made by many disabled people between what is described as the medical model of disability and the social model.

Models of disability

The medical model is the most common view held today. In essence it maintains that disabled people should be 'treated', 'changed', 'improved' and made more 'normal'. The medical model identifies what doctors see as disabled people's problems and sets about using various forms of therapy and medical intervention to make the disabled person better able to cope with and fit into the world as it stands.

On the other hand, the social model suggests that it is the world which needs changing. If the physical environment were designed for all to use, including people with disabilities, and social attitudes were correspondingly changed—in other words, all barriers to a full life removed—no one would need to feel disabled by the world in which they lived. A film was once made which illustrated the point cleverly. It was set in a world in which all doorways and entrances were designed for wheelchair users. They only had to be four foot tall. It was the 'able-bodied' people who were disabled by the environment, having to stoop or bend to get through every entrance.

There is one further aspect of the image of disability which involves disabled people's perception of themselves. This is best illustrated by looking at one disability which frequently results in

16

little or no physical restrictions or problem in coping with the environment, and yet is in reality very disturbing to the individual: disfigurement. James Partridge, who was severely burned in a car accident at the age of eighteen in 1970, underwent lengthy plastic surgery to his face. He had to cope not only with finding his familiar and acceptable looks totally changed, but also with the reactions of other people: friends, family and the public. He refers to disfigurement having two dimensions, which in his book *Changing Faces* he describes as the personal and social dimensions.

> They indicate the change that you have to go through in becoming disfigured, and how you are seen by others.
>
> 'Personal disfigurement' refers to the change that takes place in your perception of yourself. The sort of mental picture you have of yourself and your body will be radically altered. Although you may possess the same eyes for seeing, voice for talking and mind for thinking, you will alter the way you think of your face.
>
> It is not just your body-image that will change but also the way you conduct and speak about yourself. If you have been previously "normal faced", you will have adopted mannerisms and habits of mind that have evolved since your early childhood. Your looks, your body language and your spoken attitudes were previously reliable guides to your character. In their place you now have a disfigured face and, as a result, massive uncertainty about how to relate to others. In effect, your personal evaluation of your own worth may well be threatened: it will be hard for you to maintain your self-respect because your face is now so blemished and battered.
>
> 'Social disfigurement' is the way in which your disfigurement will be viewed in the eyes of others. Your facial oddities will now mark you out as different, and you will, without any choice, join the ranks of the 'handicapped' in society. What this means is that you now have a very conspicuous and, as seen in the eyes of others, debilitating trait that makes it difficult for them to behave normally with you. They may bring assumptions about 'the disfigured' as a whole to bear when deciding how best to behave with you.

However, to return to my own narrative, I came into contact with new ideas, new interests and professional concerns relating to disability in its widest sense. They did not take over from my interests in religious affairs, but supplemented and complemented them. One consequence has been that over these four years, I have became aware how little thought is given by religious thinkers and leaders to the issues of justice and rights articulated by disabled people. Yet I have also become aware, in that time, of how little there is in the expanding literature by disabled people that addresses the fundamental theological questions: Why do people have differing physical abilities? Does disability have a purpose and meaning? The Christian faith in particular has a developed philosophy of suffering, and yet has done little to translate it into terms which might mean something to a disabled person. Indeed many disabled people would argue that the concept of suffering is irrelevant. The controversial Australian comedian Steady Eddy, when asked did he view himself as a cerebral palsy sufferer, replied 'Yes, if earning A$350,000 is suffering.'

Faith and disability

Those exploring questions of faith will always miss an important dimension if they neglect to investigate and learn from the insights of disabled people. For instance, many people with disabilities are faced day by day with their own mortality. I know of one man whose breathing needs to be assisted day in, day out by an electric pump. When this stops he has to raise an alarm; he knows that unless help arrives and there is someone to pump his breathing apparatus manually until the electric pump is fixed, he has only minutes, sometimes seconds, to live. There are parents too who, against all expectations—particularly their own—have bonded in the deepest possible way with their profoundly disabled children. They also have many things to teach the church about living on the border of life and death, and on the fine boundary which separates a seemingly purposeful from a supposedly purposeless existence. Yet seldom if ever are they consulted by the churches or by theologians looking for an understanding of the divine will. And rarely do religious thinkers contemplating the Gospel imperatives ask disabled people about their perceptions of Christianity.

Except in a few cases, where disabled people are fully active as themselves within a church community, there appears to be little equal exchange of information. True, many people inspired by religious faith care for and care deeply about some profoundly disabled 'patients'. But it is frequently a one-way relationship between the carer and the cared for. What, for instance, do caring Christians make of the words of the Gospel that it is more blessed to give than to receive? Many disabled people have no option but to spend a life receiving care, simply in order to live. They are expected to be constantly grateful. Are they also expected to believe that they are less blessed because they always have to be on the receiving end?

Through this book I hope to bring together the two areas of professional interest in which I have specialized, to make sense of both by drawing on the lessons of both. I cannot pretend to have come to any major or profound conclusions but rather presenting arguments and the range of points of view, I hope that I will be able to highlight the areas where a pooling of experience and insight would be of value to many.

In particular I hope that the book may articulate some of the anxieties and confusions felt by individual disabled people. To live with a disability often imposes additional stress. Often these stresses stem from practical considerations, money, mobility, continence or whatever. Usually there is practical advice available to help people overcome the difficulties which carers and others talk about openly and are prepared to face. The answers they produce may not be satisfactory, but at least the questions can be openly considered. Knowing about and claiming all one's benefits does not add up to a decent living, yet there are people at hand prepared to talk about such things and offer what advice they can.

However, considerable emotional stress can build up for many people because there is no specialist or practitioner, counsellor or friend they feel they can trust enough to understand their many unfocused concerns. Disability can, as a result, produce confusion, depression and guilt. 'Why has this happened to me?' quickly becomes 'What use am I now?' Some people mask an inner turmoil with a brave jolly exterior. Others may channel frustration and anger into political action.

Everyone goes through life with unanswered questions. Some people refuse to face these questions until at the bitter end they are forced to. But disability puts these sharp fundamental questions into focus. There are no definitive answers, but there seem to be few open channels of discussion either. And all this applies to carers as well—especially family members whose lives are entirely shaped by the needs of a disabled parent or child.

The church's response

Church teaching, it would appear, is still largely rooted in what the radical disabled people see as outdated modes of thinking. There are many laudable Christian organizations and charities providing care, but not, the new disabled lobby would argue, advocating independence and pride for disabled people. There are active healing ministries, and in some quarters much emphasis is placed on amazing miracles, yet many disabled radicals, especially those with disabilities from birth, say this is to miss the point. They do not want to be chasing a will-o-the-wisp miracle cure, not only because it drains energy to spend a lifetime pursuing a fruitless quest, but because it undermines their own sense of pride in being who they are. Many disabled people are proud to be who they are, and they do not wish society, even in the form of well-intentioned Christians, to impose other concepts of 'normality' upon them. They do not see themselves as substandard human beings, God's mistakes. If they were to put their view theologically they would say that the Christian claim that human beings are made in God's image applies to them as much as to the able-bodied.

There are some rare cases of these views being put in this way, one of the most notable being the Canadian theologian Dr Mary Weir who talks of her deafness as a gift and part of the image of God in her.

Mary Weir however is an exception. It seems to me that church leaders are, in the main, unaware of the current thinking at the forefront of the disability movement. Yet it also seems to me that the church should be aware of this thinking and be taking immediate steps to examine it in the light of Christian theology and incorporate these new insights into church teaching. I would make one further observation: should Christian theologians start this examination, it may become painfully obvious that many of the popular and more damaging notions of disability can be traced back to Christian teaching in the past.

Is this too extreme a view? Can blame be laid at the church's door? It is certainly not an easy view to assimilate, yet it is growing in credibility and becoming far more widely held. Chapter 8 looks at some of these long-held views and discusses their faithfulness to the original biblical material.

I should add at this stage that it would be unfair to suggest that churches have totally ignored the new disability agenda. In Britain, for instance, there is an organization called Church Action on Disability (CHAD) which is not only setting out to deal with certain practical issues of how disabled people might become more involved in church life, but is also beginning to get to grips with some of the deeper issues.

CHAD is not so much an organization as a network of people from around the country, mostly people with disabilities who are trying to get the churches more aware of disability issues. It is setting out to look not only at the physical accessibility of church buildings but also at how accessible church life, work and ministry is to people with disabilities.

In the words of the Revd John Peirce, CHAD's co-ordinator speaking on the programme 'Does He Take Sugar?' in 1994:

I think there is also the issue of intellectual access, if you like to call it that. What goes on in church needs to be made intelligible to people who do not read easily or cannot hear easily, we want to understand access very widely and lead on then to participation.

Nancy Robertson, herself a wheelchair user, has direct experience of inaccessible church buildings which she described on the same programme. She now chairs CHAD but took up John Peirce's point to show how CHAD's horizons looked beyond the obvious issues of accessibility.

I think we're trying to show the contribution that people with all kinds of disabilities can make to the life of the church in the broadest sense. So often people are on the receiving end. All churches I'm sure, are anxious to do their best to involve people and show kindness and Christian charity and all the rest but so often people aren't allowed to make a contribution of what they're able to do.

There's no reason at all why people can't be involved on church councils. They could run the Sunday school, they can be readers in the church, we have members who do all of those things and indeed we have quite a number of people who are actually involved in the ministry of the church and that's something we're working on with colleges to smooth some of the barriers that prevent people training for the ministry in the various churches.

Two other members of CHAD spoke of the invisible barriers within the church which prevented disabled people from participating fully and tentatively suggested how they as disabled Christians perceived their special contribution.

Of course there are physical barriers, stairs and the like and a lack of choice as to where you can sit, but there are also attitudinal problems due to people's ignorance. They think that because you are a wheelchair user or that you're unable to see, that your brain doesn't function either and unless we make people aware of the fact that we are human beings like them we won't get past that stage.

The value of people with disabilities to the church is underestimated due to the fact that people have only really come out into the open in the last twenty years. Up until then disabled people were not seen and we as a race are very slow to change our ideas.

Disabled people are here and have things to offer. We have gifts to offer within the ministry and the church is missing out when disabled people are not participating fully within church life.

As individuals we have our own insights. As disabled people we have insights. Ultimately you could say that God has glorified a weakness, for that is the way the world sees disabled people, *as being weak. It's through that that God can use disabled people, which I believe is saying that we're there for the church to use us to show God's glory.*

This notion of God glorifying a weakness is not a theological description of disability which would gain universal acceptance, but the fact that it is articulated illustrates the wide diversity of understanding which exists to be explored. There can be no party line, no easy-to-learn dogma on the issue, for all disabled people approach the deeper meaning and issues surrounding their condition as the unique individuals they are.

2

RIGHTS NOT CHARITY

Disabled people are now refusing to accept what they need for ordinary living as a charitable gesture offered by society. They are claiming that they have the right to be taken as seriously with their needs and opinions as other sections of society, rather than to be labelled as the permanent outsiders, dependent on the kindness of others, even labelled as substandard by the way language is used.

It started as a low-key demonstration on the pavement in Whitehall outside the Department of Health. A few dozen people, many of them in wheelchairs, held up placards and chanted, 'What do we want? Civil rights! When do we want them? Now!'

A group of MPs mingling with the protesters crossed the road with a small delegation to Downing Street to deliver a protest letter to the Prime Minister. The mood was one both of anger and of an unexpected euphoria. For just a few days earlier, in that summer of 1994, a move by the Conservative Party, using some rather dubious parliamentary tactics, to kill off a bill designed to outlaw discrimination against disabled people had catapulted a minor political issue into front page headlines.

The chanting continued for a while and then, as if on cue, a group of militants edged off the pavement onto the highway and within seconds had halted two buses and a line of traffic. A policeman, who only minutes earlier had radioed his control to report a peaceful and trouble-free event, called for assistance. Soon the Parliament Square-bound lane of Whitehall was entirely blocked. A woman lay in front of the bus refusing to move, three other people had manoeuvred their wheelchairs to make it impossible for the buses to proceed even a yard. Another group of protesters had gathered around the rear of the bus on the inside lane and one had somehow become chained to it. The police mood changed as reinforcements arrived. Officers became brusque and unsympathetic. One of the demonstrators was lifted into the back of a police van. His wheelchair was left behind on the pavement.

'Last time I was in a protest,' one of the militants observed with some pride and satisfaction, 'we were treated courteously and carefully, now the police treat us like real political demonstrators.'

At the start of this century militant campaigners in Whitehall were demanding votes for women. In due course the franchise was extended and an unjust barrier to women being full participants in the democratic process was removed. In the sixties in London, though more particularly in America, the civil rights issue at the top of the agenda involved race. There is now a Race Relations Act on the statute books, apartheid has been abolished in South Africa and black African-Americans have had all legal obstacles to promotion removed. Reforming attitudes takes longer, but the legal framework to create a just society in these respects is in place.

The civil rights issue of the nineties concerns disabled people, who see themselves as having been for centuries marginalized, disregarded and even abused by society at large.

As I suggested earlier, it is an issue which many able-bodied people have not recognized and do not accept to be a civil rights question, for it challenges so many deep-seated assumptions and prejudices that the able-bodied find it hard to cope with. Even the terms used to define the issue are loaded with meaning, both good and bad.

For so long the word 'disability' has been used exclusively as a negative term. It is the very opposite of 'ability'. It challenges not only the ingrained assumptions of generations, but also the brave new world of political correctness: what words *should* properly be used to describe that state of being in which people find themselves unable to use one or more of the faculties which are normally the right of a human being?

But many would argue that phrasing the question in that way is an affront to the dignity of disabled people, who are equally human beings made in God's image, who are only defined as being different by others in the society in which they live.

One key question identified earlier which needs facing within the Christian context is this: what is meant by normality? If we are all unique creatures of God, as Christians affirm, normality becomes a meaningless concept, yet standards of normality are used day in day out by the caring professions. The first thing the parents of a newborn baby wants to know is if the child is normal: 'Does it have all its fingers and toes?' And this question is asked over and over again as the child develops. The regular check-ups given as a matter of course at health centres following the birth of a new child concentrate on measuring, weighing and assessing development. Parents are told constantly that their babies are behaving normally, or are the right weight within the normal parameters. They naturally worry if they are told that their child is a few weeks late in walking, and feel proud if he or she is a few weeks in advance of the normal age for uttering the first few words. The idea of normality fixed in the mind is rarely questioned.

This idea was once very starkly challenged, however, on one edition of 'Does He Take Sugar?' by a German delegate to a European conference on disability. She had been born without arms and, using mouth and feet, had learned how to do everything she needed to do in life. She had rebelled against those who, during her childhood, had attempted to get her to wear prosthetic arms, though she was punished for refusing to wear them. She was fiercely proud of who she was.

But if you had a child, she was asked, when he or she was born would you not ask the usual question: Is my child normal?

Her reply was quite disconcerting. She said that she would want her baby to have no arms like herself. She had no reason to be ashamed of who she was and like everybody else she hoped to create a child in her own image! More on this later.

Few would identify with such a forthright view, yet on the other hand, it is possible to argue that to talk of people being 'normal or deviating from the normal' is not consistent with Christian teaching. It is to undermine the essential uniqueness of every individual. A more acceptable word to use might be 'average'. It is possible to talk without stigma about people of average height. Problems might emerge where the deviation from the mean is too extreme and care has to be taken when talking about people being 'below average intelligence', but the term has useful potential as a neutral frame of reference for diagnosis. A doctor, for instance, might be alerted by a child failing to maintain an average growth pattern or failing to walk by the average time at which walking is achieved. However, the term also has its drawbacks. If there were one hundred people in a room and one had had a leg amputated, the average number of legs per person in that group would be 1.99. Using figures like this can lead to absurdity!

Classification

At one stage in history, scientific classification was all the rage. As the amazing diversity of the natural world was being discovered scientists felt impelled to describe and classify everything that was discovered. Every plant from the New World was given a new Latin name, every animal, from mammal to humblest insect, had to be fitted into its place in what the scientists saw as the natural order. Similarly, doctors studying people with disabilities were often more interested in defining 'abnormalities' and naming syndromes than in treating their disabled patients as individuals whose special needs they might have been able to meet. There are dusty medical tomes full of collections of pictures of human beings, now long dead, who were defined according to the fashionable labels of the time as 'idiots', 'cretins' or 'mongols'.

Regrettably this approach has not been entirely eliminated from medical training. Although offensive terminology may have been eradicated, medical students are still today shown rare classifications of 'abnormality' with unedifying enthusiasm. Patients with rare conditions are well used to being invited to sit in lecture halls before rows of aspiring doctors or asked to give their consent to be prodded by dozens of eager fingers. What one might assume as the essentials of medical training, such as teaching new doctors how to minimize the devastating effect of telling a patient of a fatal condition, are still ignored or sidelined. Nevertheless medical students are encouraged to see and note rare and exotic conditions they are most unlikely ever to encounter as general practitioners.

In the old, but not so long ago, days, the lame, the blind, the cripples were all given their place, and correctly labelled in the medical dictionaries. Today this concept of classification still persists in certain areas. In such movements as the Paralympic Games, for instance, sportsmen and women with cerebral palsy, for example, have to demonstrate to a medical panel the exact nature of their disability before being given a classification in which they can compete.

This might appear to be the sensible thing to do in order to give every competitor an equal chance of winning, yet classification is not that simple. It frequently implies either status or stigma and too frequently, for a person with a disability, it has meant stigma.

Once the term 'handicap' was employed as the gentle way of describing a person who was crippled. However, it is now an unsatisfactory term. In English it is seen to imply dependence, that a person needs to go 'cap in hand' to society to be granted a living. Interestingly, the term does not have the same scope for mis-interpretation in French, where to talk of someone being handicapped is acceptable everyday speech. Today, in English 'disabled' is a preferred expression, but to lump everyone with a disability together as 'the disabled' is not considered correct. This is to imply that 'the disabled' are a category of their own, somehow apart from society, and not to be treated as individuals with the same rights and duties as everyone else.

A recent code of practice for the media (of which more in Chapter 3), drawn up by RADAR, reserved some of its strongest words for the way in which language can create stigma and submerge individual dignity. It considers that the word 'handicapped' carries powerful associations of disabled people as passive objects of charity rather than active individuals. The word 'invalid' RADAR suggests could also give the impression that the person is 'not valid'. It says that all collective terms such as 'the disabled' or 'the blind' are to be avoided.

There is, however, a fine line to be drawn between avoiding language which stereotypes and being obsessively politically correct. PC became fashionable in the United States some ten years ago and particularly in the hands of some interest groups has become something of a joke.

In the field of disability the word 'challenged' has been introduced as a suffix to convey a personal disadvantage in a more positive light. However, this usage has been taken up more in humour than in serious discussion.

In 1986 the American journal *Publishers Week* introduced a new diet book as a 'comprehensive fitness program for the physically challenged'. And in his witty *Politically Correct Phrasebook* Nigel Rees admits that actual PC '-challenged' coinages are now far outnumbered by jocular inventions. He gives some examples:

◆ trichologically challenged = bald
◆ chronologically challenged = old
◆ hygienically challenged = dirty
◆ aesthetically challenged = ugly
◆ metabolically challenged = dead.

His entry in the same book for 'disabled' says

There is no aspect of political correctness more challenging than in deciding which words should be used to describe the mentally and physically disabled. When I invited Marlene Pease, producer of BBC Radio's long-running programme 'Does He Take Sugar?', to give me her comments on this highly-charged field, she said: 'The language used to describe disability and disabled people is politically volatile and changing so fast that it is almost impossible to keep up... It is almost impossible to get the terminology right—what suits one person doesn't suit another.'

The whole debate about language has come about, as late twentieth-century liberals have agonized over a collective cultural guilt. Some disabled people see radical correctness as patronizing and dishonest, a hypocritical attempt to change the superficial without radically reassessing the deep-seated prejudices and fears which exist in society. Others have used explosive tactics to blow open the charade. The most politically incorrect expressions are hijacked by disabled people themselves and worn as a badge of honour. Some young people with cerebral palsy refer to each other as spastics, knowing the irony of using the word. Other disabled people have reintroduced 'cripple' to the vocabulary.

The challenges of disability

However, in spite of over-the-top PC language, the notion of challenge is worth persisting with. Everyone in life has a disability of one sort or another, therefore each one of us is presented with challenges in life. Jesus' parable of the talents illustrates this well. An employer gave each one of his employees a set amount of money, measured in the old currency of the talent, to invest while he went away. The most enterprising employees took the opportunity to make more money out of the initial sum given. The least enterprising, the one ultimately condemned, was the one who buried his talent in the ground for safety and did not attempt to make the most of the opportunities offered.

Life is a succession not only of hurdles but of opportunities. Indeed, each hurdle can be an opportunity. Disability, whatever form it takes, at whatever stage it strikes, is both a hurdle and a challenge. It can also be a temptation to bury one's talents, to refuse to face up to the potential of one's disabilities; there are many disabled people who do just that. They wallow in their own self-pity. They become difficult people to know and then complain about why no one wants to know them.

The 'challenge' of disability is not an idea that comes readily to mind to the patient, newly injured, lying at Stoke Mandeville with a crushed spine and a restricted life of tetraplegia ahead. Or to the mother who, having given birth in love and pain, is told, often in a rather embarrassed and gauche way, by the nursing staff, that there is something 'not quite right' about her child.

But it has another meaning too. Disability also challenges the people who consider themselves able-bodied.

Society is riddled with prejudice. On the one hand, disabled people are fitted into stereotypes. Even in films it is still the practice to portray evil through disability. Hunchbacked dwarfs and men with hooks or stumps for limbs are all too readily used to convey negative, evil and malicious images. Just think of the 'cut-out' villains of the James Bond films!

On the other hand, disability can often produce a cloying, patronizing response which diminishes disabled people in their own and in society's eyes as individuals. For years there has been a strong lobby amongst disabled people calling for the banning of the television 'Telethon' and 'Children in Need' appeals. Such media events have, it is said, required disabled people to prostitute their disabilities in front of the cameras as part of a new form of electronic-age begging. Is it not often the case that able-bodied people try to salve their own consciences by giving money to collectors dressed up in funny clothes, and think that by doing so they have met their obligations? Think too of the commercial companies whose PR men and women make public presentations of cheques—often spending more on the giving than the gift. Charity makes many disabled people very uneasy.

No wonder, then, that the slogan used by charity protesters, like those who recently gathered outside the House of Commons lobbying for the Civil Rights Disabled Person's Bill, is 'rights not charity'.

Public attitudes

'Rights not charity' may be a simple slogan, but the purpose of the new generation of civil rights is far more complex. Indeed many will have not seen beyond the basic civil rights issues of being given equal opportunities in employment and equal access to public buildings and transport. They are not content with being obedient and subservient; they do not see it as their role to be grateful recipients, to stay out of sight and cause no trouble. The questions they raise are uncomfortable ones which go to the very root of our society and its Christian heritage. They are unleashing a turmoil of emotions which many people will find hard to cope with. Society's subjugation of disabled people has not been brought about by any innate cruelty or lust for power, but by the inability of most people to face the basic and discomforting questions raised by disability, in a culture in which the promise of physical human perfection is always presented as the ideal, even the totem of the age.

It is very sobering to recall how malleable these emotions are. There is ample evidence to suggest that when leaders do lust after power and are unashamed of their innate cruelty, the fears and ideals of ordinary people can be shockingly manipulated. It cannot be forgotten that the victims of the Holocaust, although primarily Jewish, also included many other minority groups. High on Hitler's list were hundreds of thousands of people with disabilities. And the Nazis succeeded in perpetrating their outrages because they knew how to play on popular sentiments and civic frailty. When times were bad economically, as they were between the wars in Germany, it was all too easy to find scapegoats in the form of the Jews and victims in the form of disabled people.

It should never be forgotten that so many thousands of disabled people were sent to the gas chambers and concentration camps. Nor should it be forgotten that although this was the most extreme example of its kind this century, the propensity to seek and condone such solutions still exists. In July 1993 Michael Lawton reported from Germany for 'Does He Take Sugar?' on certain unpleasant incidents in which disabled people were targeted.

A visually handicapped man was beaten to death on his way home from work by two skinheads. A mentally disabled man was held prisoner for four days and tortured; four deaf children were beaten up as the public looked on. In one town a mentally disabled man was beaten and told that the disabled had no place in Germany.

Michael Lawton attended a rally in which several hundred people demonstrated against this new wave of violence. It was there that he met Frank Weber, a wheelchair user from Cologne, who told him of his own experience of how the climate was changing.

I was in a department store, I wanted to buy a concert ticket and while I was waiting three neo-Nazis came up to me, one from each side and one from the front. They were wearing swastikas and leather jackets and boots and they started inciting me. One of them said, 'What do you want here? They must have forgotten to deal with you in Dachau.' At first I was completely shocked and when I got over the shock I decided to go to the newspapers and the television and I also helped to organize a candlelight vigil in Cologne.

Michael Lawton reported another firsthand case of a German disabled person feeling the neo-Nazi backlash. The disabled man's wife recounted the story of what happened one day as she cycled behind him as he rode his tricycle along a narrow bike path in their home town near Hanover. It was early afternoon and school had just come out.

First the boy stepped into his path. I thought it was an accident, that he had slipped and then as we went on I saw that the boys were spitting at him and saying, 'You live off our taxes, you'd have been gassed under Hitler.' It went on and on. I couldn't understand why my husband rode on, but he looked straight ahead and just drove straight on until they couldn't follow us. And then I saw for the first time how he was covered in spit and I wiped him and he said that he was so sorry that I had to find out about it, but I shouldn't be sad, it wasn't new to him. He said it was the first time for me but it had happened to him often and it didn't matter to him.

But the truth is that it did matter to him. Shortly afterwards the man committed suicide. He wrote in his farewell letter to his wife that 'disabled people do not have a chance in this world any more'.

It appears in Germany, with serious cuts being made in the benefits received by disabled people, that many are feeling increasingly insecure. Will they eventually be placed in institutions rather than be allowed to live independently in the community? Coupled with that insecurity are the stories about violence to disabled people. The Commissioner for Disabled People's Affairs in Lower Saxony has been gathering letters from disabled people describing their experiences.

This new climate is causing people to say that they are frightened, frightened even though nothing has happened to them yet. But people also write to me to tell me of attacks on their abilities to live independent lives. It's sad for example that we can't provide disabled access for the tram because we need the money to rebuild East Germany or when local residents don't want a school for children with learning difficulties in their area because of the noise or when disabled people at the seaside are told to get out of sight. I want to point out that it's not just in East Germany, it's not just right-wing youth. It's normal citizens who through their behaviour exclude disabled people from participation in society.

Perhaps the most notorious example was when a German court allowed a family to claim back part of the cost of its package holiday on the grounds that their enjoyment was spoiled by the presence of disabled people in their dining-room.

And disabled people in Germany have no protection from the law, for while Paragraph 3 of the German Constitution prohibits discrimination on grounds of sex, race, religion, politics and origin it does not include discrimination on grounds of disability. That is one of the demands being made by German disabled activists for they point to the existence of the prohibitions against discrimination in the German Constitution as a direct historical consequence of the need after the Second World War to protect people who were persecuted under the Third Reich. They did not include disabled people because fifty years ago there was no awareness of this discrimination and the need to provide protection.

The current climate in Germany has also rekindled the debate on euthanasia. Indeed under the Nazis the first gas chambers were developed to carry out a programme of euthanasia singling out disabled people. Today, with this tradition in mind disabled people in Germany fear the effect of a book like *Should the baby live?* co-authored by the Australian moral philosopher Peter Singer. In Germany this book is particularly controversial. Invitations issued to Singer to speak at German universities were withdrawn and the publication of the book postponed.

The book argues that in certain cases it might be legal to actively kill infants whose life chances are seen by parents and doctors to be minimal. To many modern Germans that sounds very close to the Nazi slogan of 'life unworthy of life'. The idea that there should be some sort of cost-benefit analysis of life chances is naturally anathema to many disabled people. The Association for the Integration of Disabled People based in Munich points out modern echoes of this philosophy. At a time of recession the issue of costs increasingly defines the lives of disabled people.

Politicians refer to old people and disabled people as 'care receivers' or as 'cost factors' and not as people. Against their will, the Association for the Integration of Disabled People argues, many will be forced to live in a certain way for reasons of cost. For example if a disabled person wants to move from one city to another it is very difficult because of the bureaucracy involved in transferring the care finance from one social services department to another. There have been such human rights violations against disabled people for a long time in Germany, the Association argues, and the press has only become interested since the right-wingers have started being violent.

In Michael Lawton's view disabled people fear that, faced with recession, the gains made by disabled people since the liberal and wealthy sixties will be rolled back. According to disabled activists, without legal protection social services could be seen as a luxury which society can only afford when things are going well. A spokesperson for the German Federation of Disabled Employers believes that things are tougher now than they were ten years ago.

Governments and people working in the disability field express their regret about the people killed because of their disabilities under the Third Reich but, say many activists, this is hypocritical because 'they don't feel sorry any more. They even accept at many levels that disabled people should be hidden and isolated in life. They are being separated to special schools and special transportation and sheltered workshops.'

However, this perspective is not acknowledged publicly by the German government. Officially it deplores the attacks on disabled people but argues that there is no more violence of that nature in Germany than in any other country, including Britain. It says the government has no indication that violence against disabled people has proportionally increased in comparison with the general level of violence. The government also points out that it has not been able to prove statistically that attacks on disabled people are coming from right-wing organizations or right-wingers.

Is the German government right? Although Nazism may have been the most unpleasant and extreme exhibition of prejudice in history, there is violence and prejudice lurking in every nation. A few extremists and politicians cannot be isolated for blame.

The UK record

How does the United Kingdom compare? The point made about disabled people being forced to live in a certain way because of cost also applies. The new Care in the Community provisions require local authorities to make assessments of each disabled person's needs. These needs should then be met in the most appropriate way for that person. In practice, however, needs are met in the way which enables the local authority to cope with its restricted budget. Many people have little choice as to when their home helps or care assistants arrive, what time they go to bed at night, where or how they go shopping. And as for moving from one city to another, similar bureau-cratic restrictions exist. Talking to one person with cerebral palsy living in a special support scheme in Milton Keynes I suggested he had a high degree of independence. 'Yes,' he replied, 'as long as you don't ever want to move from Milton Keynes.'

To understand these phenomena further it is worth exploring the way in which disabled people are seen by society, especially through the mass media. For it is the mass media that not only reflect but form attitudes. It will be seen that in many subtle ways disabled people are kept out of the mainstream and individual disabled people with much to offer are marginalized and discounted by being classified as disabled.

The ultimate consequences for those concerned might not be as brutal and as savage as experienced by those who suffered under the pogroms instigated by Hitler but the consequences can, nevertheless, be devastating to an individual's life chances and choices. It is a fact of the human condition, not just restricted to Germany, that people look for scapegoats to blame in times of stress. Similarly people, especially in groups, need to find another group not just to blame but to look down upon. It is the people with the least power in society, with the weakest forms of defence, who so often fit the bill.

If discrimination or prejudice against disabled people is seen in this light, the Christian message is clear. Christians are expected to treat those seen as the least important not only as they would expect to be treated themselves by others, but as if they were dealing with Christ himself. To which many will reply, but we do. We make a point of talking to people in wheelchairs, of giving money to charity, supporting the Children in Need appeal. They are thankful they are not as others are, those who might pass by on the other side when they see the charity collector, who never take the arm of the blind person standing on the edge of the road. But here lies the true challenge of disability for society. Many disabled people will argue they want to be treated as people with rights, not objects of charity or curiosity; I am sure the blind friend of mine who tells this story is not unique.

He was waiting in the High Street of his local town for his wife, who had just gone into a shop. He knew the area well and positioned himself on the pavement nearby to wait for her. Suddenly he felt someone grab his arm. He wondered if he was being kidnapped. He was so surprised that before he could manage to say, 'What on earth are you doing?' he had been whisked to the other side of the street and dumped. 'Just doing my good deed for the day,' said a cheery voice disappearing into the distance.

3

IMAGE

Our image of disability is largely gained from the mass media, unless we have personal experience of it. These images and the word pictures used to describe disabled people can be more 'crippling' for them than their physical or mental condition, and can obscure rather than communicate the truth.

Two years ago the results of a survey were published. It looked at the way in which disabled people were being portrayed on television, the main medium today whereby attitudes are created and prejudices confirmed. The survey was based around the work of the Broadcasting Research Unit and the conclusions were written up by Guy Cumberbatch and Ralph Negrine. They discovered that during the course of their monitoring of programmes, people with disabilities appeared in 16 per cent of all factual programmes and 24 per cent of news programmes, yet over the same period not one of the 44 game shows observed contained a single person with a disability.

The most common focus for factual reporting involving people with disabilities was medical treatment, with the second most common focus being on the 'special achievement' of the disabled person. The overwhelming line taken in reviewing medical treatment and disability involved finding a cure for the condition. When it came to fictional programmes people with disabilities represented 0.5 per cent of all the characters portrayed. This contrasts with the evidence of official statistics which suggest that

14 per cent of the adult population of Britain has a disability of one kind or another, although not all disabilities are visible, and comparing the two figures involves making allowances for this.

Of course, it was not only disabled people who were represented in a disproportionate manner. The same programmes analyzed showed that 65 per cent of all characters were male, 95 per cent white and over 50 per cent in the narrow age band of twenty-five to forty. The unit's analysis of feature films produced evidence that when disabled people are portrayed it is as stereotypes and the disabled person is shown 'as a criminal or only barely human or someone who is powerless and pathetic'. The unit came to a damning conclusion that the characters with disabilities were included in the story lines for ulterior motives.

That is, not because they are ordinary people who one might expect to encounter in an ordinary society, to the contrary, they would appear to be brought in to enhance the atmosphere of a film when it needs to be one of deprivation or mystery or menace. In short, disabled characters are introduced not because they are ordinary people like others but in order to suggest precisely the opposite, that they are not ordinary people.

Media images

To many people television is not viewed critically and is not seen to present a distorted view of the real world. On the contrary it is supposed to represent the real world itself! If one's horizons are only extended by television, and one's life experience, apart from one's family, workplace and neighbourhood, is made up entirely of images from the screen, then the television producer's image of the world becomes particularly powerful. Obviously at a superficial level viewers distinguish between fact and fiction, but at the subliminal level television is a powerful reinforcer of the image that society is a place for and peopled by ideal human beings—the presentable, the healthy and the 'normal'.

A similar analysis of newspaper photographs was made, in conjunction with an exhibition of public images of disability. The results were similar to those of the television unit. Disabled people were categorized either as superheroes or as pathetic victims. The image was frequently reinforced that disabled people were suffering from a medical condition which had somehow distorted their real selves. Amongst popular press stories and pictures were those showing how medical science was advancing. These stories emphasized how through medical research, it would be possible in future years to identify many disabilities at an early stage so that they could be eradicated.

A study published recently by the Spastics Society entitled *What the papers say and don't say about disability* described how the language used to portray people with physical or mental disabilities was often pejorative and prejudicial, while news important to disabled people was often suppressed in favour of sensational tales of individual suffering. The coverage by newspapers of disability only in medical and individual terms, the study claimed, reinforced stereotypes. The four-week study monitoring tabloids and broadsheets found in the main medical stories which portrayed disabled people as suffering victims waiting for miracle cures. Words such as 'abnormality' and 'deformity', the study said, implied that disabled people could never be happy or fulfilled.

This general view is supported by the group ParentAbility, part of the National Childbirth Trust which supports parents with disabilities. It was the organization behind the exhibition of photographs and it reviewed not just newspaper photographs but those appearing in the glossy magazines and in advertisements. In material accompanying the exhibition the point was made strongly that few photographs are ever published showing disabled people caring for children.

The image of disabled people on charity posters, alone and socially 'out of it' could hardly be further away from the image of the harassed parent 'in the thick of it' and weighed down by tasks and responsibilities. Parents care and disabled people are cared for. Isn't that how it is?

So ParentAbility set about building up a stock of images for newspapers to use of disabled people as parents and grandparents.

The organization now has a picture archive but is fully aware of one difficulty. When it comes to raising money, charities still feel that they need to reinforce the public image of the disabled person in need in order to maximize income. Money is still required for many basic things which the state does not provide and charity fund-raisers feel that if the image of disabled people becomes one of independence and coping with the world, income might be reduced.

Able-bodied people should perhaps put themselves in the place of the disabled viewer. Here he or she is watching television for entertainment and information, believing it to be a fair reflection of society. Yet on all those happy optimistic shows there is no one like themselves. Whenever someone like themselves is shown it is to represent some negative idea. You feel it difficult to identify with that society if that is the way that society feels about you. And yet you cannot opt out. The depressing conclusion you come to is that the attitudes you experience day by day do not just stem from unthinking or uncaring individuals, but are condoned by the community at large.

As for self-image, television and the print media are profoundly destructive. The power of the standard image of the body beautiful—tall, slender, youthful—wreaks havoc with self-esteem. So much so that many disabled people conclude in desperation that disability and ugliness must be synonymous.

This notion is sharply contradicted by a group of Liverpool-based disabled fashion models now making their way in the world. They are wheelchair users whose poise and physical charisma make a profound visual impact.

Aware, nevertheless, of the power and tendencies of the media to distort the image of disability, the Royal Association of Disability And Rehabilitation (RADAR) has drawn up a code of practice to guide those involved in the press, radio and television. With statistics showing that almost one in ten of the population is disabled, and experience confirming that there is no clear dividing line between being able-bodied and disabled, with everyone possessing ranges of ability to differing degrees of disability, the code of practice is designed to focus the attention of journalists, producers and others away from seeing 'the disabled' as a special group and towards seeing everyone in society as an individual. Disability has been described as a very ordinary part of life; it is the commonly accepted myths and stereotypes about disabled people, frequently reinforced by the media, which make disability seem an extraordinary thing; and RADAR says that it would be hard to overestimate the damage caused by the media's frequent repetition of negative images of disabled people.

One of the key areas focused on by RADAR in its advice to the media is the way in which the media make assumptions or generalizations about the way disabled people feel. Many people, says RADAR, simply regard the difficulties associated with their disabilities as a normal part of life. To describe them as sufferers is both inaccurate and patronizing. Nevertheless newspaper accounts are still full of references to 'cerebral palsy sufferers' and 'the wheelchair-bound disabled'.

So RADAR's advice to journalists is to avoid describing an individual person as 'a victim of', 'crippled by' or 'afflicted by' a disability. It suggests replacing 'confined to a wheelchair' with 'wheelchair user', as from the point of view of the user the wheelchair is an aid to mobility and not a restriction.

The writer Quentin Crewe, now a wheelchair user, describes vividly how he realized at each stage of his life, as his mobility decreased, how aids to mobility gave new freedoms to him, not restrictions. He graduated from walking unsteadily to using a stick, to using a wheelchair, to using a powered wheelchair. When each moment came to make a switch he discovered a new liberty, and realized how restricted he had been by hanging on to the inappropriate mobility aid for too long.

RADAR makes the point strongly that disabled people should not be stereotyped as heroes or victims. Andy Berry, an active member of the Spastics Society (recently renamed SCOPE in an attempt to overcome the negative associations of the word 'spastic'), who himself has cerebral palsy, tells the story of how he was once telephoned by a journalist wanting to write a story about the computer company he ran. After a while the journalist said, 'Do you mind me asking but are you disabled?' Andy Berry could not deny the fact; his speech gave it away. Yet as soon as that fact was established Andy feared for the worst and indeed his fears were not groundless. The story which appeared was not focused on the achievements of the company but on those of Andy, cerebral palsy 'hero' businessman.

To be fair to journalists and editors, it was not the modern media which created the current image of disability. Modern media simply reinforce an old set of notions using modern technology. The negative image of disability has existed for centuries and, even though individual disabled people have throughout history triumphed against the odds, in some cases so successfully that the disability was barely noticed, the lot of the majority has been far from happy. Frequently in the past amputees and people with physical malformations have had to resort to humiliating prostitution of their disabilities in order to live. Some became professional beggars, others joined freak shows. However an even greater number were simply locked away—out of sight and mind of the general public.

For not only was stereotyping commonplace but the fears generated by disability were nearer the surface than today. Over and over again, in looking at the great literature of the past, that fear was reinforced—or perhaps one should say, given voice—by equating disability with evil. In Shakespeare's *Richard III* Richard Duke of Gloucester, later to become King Richard III, is seen at the start of Act I in London introducing himself. Shakespeare has no qualms about portraying him as a figure of darkness and wickedness and using a physical disability for all its dramatic effect. The hunchback king limps malevolently onto the stage and opens the play with the famous words, 'Now is the winter of our discontent made glorious summer by this sun of York...' But before long he is describing himself as curtailed of fair proportion, 'cheated of feature by dissembling nature, deformed, un-finished, sent before my time into this breathing world, scarce half made up, and that so lamely and unfashionable that dogs bark at me as I halt by them.'

Dickens and disability

Two days before Christmas 1993, 'Does He Take Sugar?' broadcast a round-table conversation explaining how Charles Dickens used and exploited images of disability, giving to his readers and subsequent generations some of the most savage, most gentle and most influential stereotypes. It was 150 years to the week since Charles Dickens had published *A Christmas Carol*, the story of

Scrooge, the three ghosts of Christmas and in particular Tiny Tim, the disabled son of Scrooge's long-suffering clerk, Bob Cratchett. Tiny Tim was one of the many characters Dickens created to whom he gave a disability for his own literary purposes. Mr Dick had learning difficulties, as we would say today; little Joe had facial disfigurements; was Barnaby Rudge perhaps autistic? Dickens also included an early wheelchair user.

What can we learn by looking at Dickens' use of disabled characters about the way attitudes have changed over the last century and a half? Discussing Dickens and disability were Dr Malcolm Andrews, a Dickens expert from the University of Kent at Canterbury and editor of *The Dickensian*, the magazine of the Dickens' Fellowship, Professor Mike Oliver, Professor of Disability Studies at the University of Greenwich, and Sally Witcher, Director of the Child Poverty Action Group and formerly of Disability Alliance.

Malcolm Andrews set the scene with a reading from *A Christmas Carol*, taken from the visit of the second of the three spirits. Scrooge sees Bob Cratchett coming home from church on Christmas Day with Tiny Tim upon his shoulder.

Alas for Tiny Tim, he bore a little crutch and had his limbs supported by an iron frame!...

'And how did little Tim behave?' asked Mrs Cratchett...

'As good as gold,' said Bob, 'and better. Somehow he gets thoughtful, sitting by himself so much, and thinks the strangest things you ever heard. He told me, coming home, that he hoped the people saw him in the church, because he was a cripple, and it might be pleasant to them to remember upon Christmas Day, who made lame beggars walk and blind men see.'

Scrooge is shown this vision by the Ghost of Christmas Present, so the story relates, to point out the error of his ways in being bad-tempered and in despising merriment and the entire Christmas spirit. A little later Scrooge sees his clerk Bob Cratchett holding Tiny Tim's withered little hand.

'Spirit,' said Scrooge, with an interest he had never felt before, 'tell me if Tiny Tim will live.'

'I see a vacant seat,' replied the Ghost, 'in the poor chimney corner, and a crutch without an owner, carefully preserved. If these shadows remain unaltered by the Future, the child will die.'

'No, no,' said Scrooge. 'Oh no, kind Spirit! say he will be spared.'

'If these shadows remain unaltered by the Future, none other of my race,' returned the Ghost, 'will find him here. What then? If he be like to die, he had better do it, and decrease the surplus population.'

Scrooge hung his head to hear his own words quoted by the Spirit, and was overcome with penitence and grief.

Even 150 years on, the Tiny Tim character can pluck the heart strings of the reader in precisely the way Dickens intended; but Sally Witcher was not so impressed.

I think I can sum it up by saying, 'Pass me the sick bag please!' It's absolutely dire! It reminds me of Telethon, of Children in Need and similar such programmes. They represent a thoroughly damaging portrayal of disabled people and also a thoroughly damaging portrayal of a response to disabled people. There's nothing in there which I would describe as positive.

Mike Oliver concurred.

It seems 150 years ago there was a desire to get rid of disabled people by curing them; there's a desire to get rid of them today by curing them also.

Malcolm Andrews then painted in the background to the famous Christmas-tide story.

Dickens was indeed deliberately using a disabled person for sentimental effect, to get the tears running down the cheeks of his readers.

The Carol itself began life not as a ghost story but as part of Dickens' aim to launch an appeal on behalf of the poor man's child. He had read a report from a parliamentary commission earlier in the year 1843, which gave a graphic account of the conditions in which the factory children were working, children generally of the poor and parish orphans and he said he was perfectly struck down by it, that he thought of launching a pamphlet appeal. He changed his mind for rather mysterious reasons, kept the whole thing quiet, but by the end of the year what became apparent was that there wasn't going to be an appeal on behalf of the poor man's child, it was going to be **A Christmas Carol,** *and right at the centre of it is this almost emblematic poor man's child, Tiny Tim.*

'The exploitation of disabled children for charitable purposes,' Mike Oliver added, 'has a long and dishonourable history.'

Tiny Tim is, of course, only one of many disabled characters conjured up by Dickens' imagination. He is one of the best known. However, some of Dickens' most poignant writing is to be found describing some of his lesser characters, and Malcolm Andrews took as an example Master Humphrey from Dickens' work *Master Humphrey's Clock.*

Dickens in 1839 wanted to start a magazine. His idea centred around a little group of rather retiring folk who would gather together of an evening and tell stories. Master Humphrey is the central figure in this group of characters and one of the first stories to be launched in **Master Humphrey's Clock** *is* **The Old Curiosity Shop.**

Master Humphrey says in introducing himself to the reader that he's a misshapen deformed old man.

I have never been made a misanthrope by this cause; I have never been stung by any insult, nor wounded by any jest upon my crooked figure; as a child I was melancholy and timid but that was because the gentle consideration paid to my misfortune sunk deep into my spirit and made me sad even in those early days.

Sally Witcher responded:

I think what he's saying there is that somehow trying to come to terms with people being nice and considerate is much more difficult than repelling all the sort of insults and abuse that you might get because when people are trying to be nice clearly it's from the best possible intentions, the fact that it's actually very painful and can be very patronizing is very much more difficult for a disabled person to cope with, speaking as a disabled person myself. Sympathy is intolerable sometimes.

Mike Oliver, however, thought that was a misinterpretation of the passage.

When he said, 'I've never been stung by any insult,' what he says before that is he refuses to apologize for being a misshapen and deformed old man and I think what he's actually saying is not 'I've never been insulted', but 'It's never bothered me; I've had insults, I've been patronized but it's never actually bothered me.'

Is it therefore the prejudices of the other people that cause the disability? Is that what Dickens suggests in a later passage, quoted by Malcolm Andrews?

Master Humphrey gives a little anecdote about a time when he was surrounded by a number of the young children, all very beautiful children in contrast to him, though he wasn't aware of the contrast and these children were poring over a picture of some angels.

There were many lovely angels in this picture and I remember the fancy coming upon me to point out which of them represented each child there and that when I had gone through all my companions I stopped and hesitated wondering which was most like me. I remember the children looking at each other and my turning red and hot and their crowding round to kiss me saying that they loved

me all the same. And then and when the old sorrow came into my dear mother's mild and tender look the truth broke upon me for the first time and I knew, while watching my awkward and ungainly sports, how keenly she had felt for her poor crippled boy.

At that point Sally Witcher felt Dickens was succeeding in getting into the mind of his character.

This is one of the few passages which are actually written from the perspective of a disabled person and what's interesting here is that it's the disabled person who is embarrassed, elsewhere it's other people who're embarrassed by the disability. But overall it seems that we are to conclude that disability is embarrassing, if not for one then for the other. I'm not sure I'd agree with that conclusion. That embarrassment still is there in the ways that disabled people will be treated and how they themselves might feel. It's not a positive response and it's not necessary but it's about people not being integrated and there being difficulties in integrating that's still very much here today, certainly.

Mike Oliver felt it was the one passage that he was actually able to identify with.

The description there of Master Humphrey realizing he was a disabled person mirrors the kind of description that many of my disabled friends who've been disabled since birth actually tell me about. How they came to realize that they were disabled; that nobody ever actually told them and that there was this one moment where they realized either that they weren't going to grow out of it or they weren't going to get better as they put it and suddenly realized—this is it, this is life. Previously they'd been protected or somehow they'd been led to believe that all this was some kind of temporary state. Then they themselves had realized, I think that's what Dickens actually captures in that passage.

So how did Dickens manage to achieve this understanding if he had no personal experience of disability? Malcolm Andrew had a suggestion:

> I suspect the reason for his ability to quite sensitively register this stems from his childhood experiences; in many ways, though he wasn't himself disabled in any way physically, psychologically he felt disabled. He felt abandoned as a child. He felt that adulthood was prematurely thrust upon him. He felt isolated and I think therefore he has this ability to enter into the mind of the child and the marginalized and the oppressed. He manages it extremely well. On the other hand when he's propagandizing for the poor, the disabled and so on he often throws up the extremely sentimentalised conventionalized portraits of these people.

Mike Oliver added:

> He's not extraordinarily insightful into the minds of disabled people elsewhere in what he writes, and as someone coming from a working-class background I certainly don't feel his portrayal of working-class characters demonstrates that he has any real empathy or experiential base on which to base them, they come out more as caricatures rather than descriptions of what it was like to be disabled or what it was like to be working class.

Sally Witcher agreed.

> That's true; his portrayal of most people in his novels, regardless of whether they're working class, disabled or what they are, come out as very caricaturized; quite grotesque.

Inevitably Dickens' portrayal of disability included characters with learning difficulties or mental illness. One of the most celebrated is Mr Dick from *David Copperfield*, who might today be described as autistic. Malcolm Andrews introduced Mr Dick.

He is living in the same house as David's aunt Betsy Trotwood in Dover and this is David's first impression of Mr Dick when he arrives as a young boy at the Dover cottage after a long journey. He can't find his aunt but looks up to the window.

The unbroken stillness of the parlour window leading me to infer after a while that she was not there, I lifted up my eyes to the window above it where I saw a florid, pleasant looking gentleman with a grey head who shot up one eye in a grotesque manner, nodded his head at me several times, shook it at me as often, laughed and went away.

And then a little later his aunt asks David what he thinks of Mr Dick.

'What d'you think of him?' says my aunt. I had some shadowy idea of endeavouring to evade the question by replying that I thought him a very nice gentleman but my aunt was not to be so put off, for she laid her work down on her lap and said, folding her hands upon it, 'O come, be direct, be as like your sister as you can and speak out.'

'Is Mr Dick, I ask because I don't know, aunt, is he at all out of his mind then?' I stammered, for I felt I was on dangerous ground.

'Not a morsel,' said my aunt.

'O indeed,' I observed faintly.

'If there's anything in the world,' said my aunt with great decision and force of manner, 'that Mr Dick is not it's that.'

I had nothing better to offer than another timid, 'Oh indeed'.

'He has been called mad,' said my aunt. 'I have a selfish pleasure in saying he has been called mad or I should not have had the benefit of his society and advice for these last ten years and upwards.'

'So long as that?', I said.

'And nice people they were who had the audacity to call him mad', pursued my aunt. 'Mr Dick is a sort of distant connection of mine, it doesn't matter how, I needn't enter into that, if it hadn't been for me his own brother would have shut him up for life, that's all.'

I'm afraid it was hypocritical in me but seeing that my aunt felt strongly on the subject I tried to look as if I felt strongly too.

'The proud fool,' said my aunt, 'because his brother was a little eccentric, though he's not half so eccentric as a good many people, he didn't like to have visible about his house and sent him away to some private asylum place, though he had been left to his particular care by their deceased father who thought him almost a natural and a wise man he must have been to think so, mad himself no doubt.'

Sally Witcher thought it was an interesting passage, but she had her doubts.

The aunt talks about how she got him as if he were some kind of object to be fought over and a great deal of squabbling had gone on and she's at great pains to talk about how useful he is and how invaluable his advice is, as if that somehow gives him some sort of value and without it he would be quite valueless. So I think there are still some problems with the passage. It certainly does over-compensate by saying that Mr Dick is all things wonderful.

Again, Malcolm Andrews filled in the background.

Dickens around the time he was writing Copperfield *had had considerable interest in the way in which the insane were looked after, institutionalized. He had been admiring the work of regimes that didn't require physical restraint and Dickens in his own magazine,* Household Words, *and I think here, in such passages, is trying to persuade his Victorian reading public to look again at the insane, not treat them as grotesques who need to be hurried away out of sight.*

To illustrate the way in which fictional characters are used to make certain points, Mike Oliver selected a passage from *Nicholas Nickelby* about Wackford Squeers and his appearance.

Mr Squeers' appearance was not prepossessing, he had but one eye and the popular prejudice runs in favour of two. The eye he had was unquestionably useful but decidedly not ornamental being of a greenish grey and in shape resembling the fanlight of a street door. The blank side of his face was much wrinkled and puckered up which gave him a very sinister appearance especially when he smiled, at which times his expression bordered closely on the villainous.

I think it illustrates that where in literature disabled people are not being portrayed as saints they're being portrayed as villains. We have Captain Ahab in Moby Dick *who only had one leg, we have Long John Silver, we have Captain Hook. Most of the villains in the James Bond novels had a disability of one kind or another and it's almost to explain their behaviour; you have to give them a context, and I suppose it's the lazy writer's way out: if you have to put their villainy in context, give them a disability. It's an easy, quick shorthand device, but it does us as disabled people no service whatsoever.*

Sally was not convinced Mike's chosen passage illustrated that point completely.

I don't know whether Mr Squeers really is described as disabled, I entirely agree with your points about the way in which disabled people very often are portrayed as villains, but Mr Squeers' one eye was unquestionably useful. There's a great deal of emphasis equally on his clothes, it's about his appearance and possibly less so about the disability, was he perhaps a villain who happened to be disabled? Rather than a disabled person who obviously because they're disabled has to be a villain?

So was Dickens equally savage on every character, disabled or not?

Sally Witcher acknowledged his integrated approach:

Certainly he was savage about a whole range of people; it wasn't just disabled people, it wasn't people from a particular class necessarily. In some instances he uses humour in a way to be really very savage indeed, but I don't think disabled people were singled out. What's interesting though is that disabled people feature a great deal in Dickens' work, in contrast to a lot of modern literature and modern media. They were actually integrated; disabled people appeared, they featured, they were part of things in a way which I don't think they are necessarily portrayed as being now.

Mike Oliver expanded on the point.

It's quite clear that up until about 1850 disabled people did live in communities, they were integrated, they may have lived lives which were fairly harsh and fairly brutal but then so did many of their non-disabled counterparts. I think it was from the middle of the nineteenth century onwards as the number of institutions grew, as they became more specialized, as they classified people into more and more categories, that disabled people were excluded from society and as a consequence of that they came to be excluded from the literature of the time.

So was it actually a form of honesty that we dare not pursue today that Dickens wrote in such brutal ways about people with disabilities?

I would say it was a reflection of the time, and I would say that when disabled people again become truly integrated into society they will again have a proper contemporary role in literature and in the media; but that will come after disabled people have achieved for themselves full integration into society and not before.

Yet how far should brutal realism be allowed to go in literature?

Dickens is at his most extreme on a description of Miss Moucher from *David Copperfield*.

> There came waddling around a sofa, a Percy dwarf of about forty or forty-five with a very large head and face, a pair of roguish grey eyes and such extremely little arms that to enable herself to lay a finger archly against her snub nose as she ogled steerforth, she was obliged to meet the finger half way and lay her nose against it. Her chin which was what is called a double chin, was so fat that it entirely swallowed up the strings of her bonnet, bow and all. Throat she had none, waist she had none, legs she had none worth mentioning for though she was more than full-sized down to where her waist would have been if she had had any, and though she terminated as human beings generally do in a pair of feet, she was so short that she stood at a common-sized chair as at a table resting a bag she carried on the seat.

Sally Witcher and Mike Oliver were unanimous in their response to it.

> *It's quite clearly designed to be funny, it's quite clearly designed to make people laugh at disability and laugh at disabled people, therefore I find it really very offensive. I mean it's successful in terms of being funny, I'm not denying that but it's none the less really quite offensive.*

> *I think it's so malicious, I've no idea of the background to the passage, but I think it's so malicious that Dickens must have had a personal interest. It must be about someone who he felt somehow had abused him or done him wrong in his life, I cannot believe that's just an attempt to provide a description of a category, I think it's more personal than that.*

Dickens certainly had a model, a chiropodist who he had once seen, although there was no evidence of any close dealings with her; however once the person in question had read the passage she threatened a libel case against him. Dickens hurriedly had to make amends and because he was writing serial fiction he was able to modify the figure of Miss Moucher so that towards the end she's regenerated as a very different kind of character.

Given all this, should Dickens be encouraged, read in schools and held up as a great author? Sally Witcher thought there was value in it.

There's a great deal to learn from it. Whether or not you read Dickens these attitudes exist, existed then and I'm afraid still exist. It actually makes a lot of sense of what is happening now. I don't think it should do but it does.

And did Mike Oliver think that people should be encouraged to read Dickens to show how little progress has been made?

If disabled people are going to achieve their civil rights there are lots more important things that they and indeed their able-bodied allies can do rather than read Dickens. I don't think the raising of disability consciousness is dependent upon long-dead white European males; I think there are more interesting words being written about the experience of disability, which eventually will be liberating for disabled people and for society.

Has Dickens got a lot to answer for? I asked Malcolm Andrews if he had created too many images and stereotypes.

He undoubtedly created a number of grotesques, but in many other ways Dickens was advanced, humane and enlightened in his attitude towards the disabled, in the way that he insisted on exposing in his fiction various kinds of disability to an audience—particularly a genteel, rather conventional middle-class Victorian audience—who were getting increasingly squeamish, who were wanting these unsavoury-looking people out of the way.

A point in Dickens' favour? Sally Witcher said she would take a lot of convincing.

Tiny Tim has a great deal to answer for, I'd be quite happy if Tiny Tim had never existed, never been written about. But generally speaking I think Dickens is worth reading because apart from anything else disabled people need to know what they're up against and that's important because we need to know where our starting point is before we can actually make progress.

Mike Oliver responded:

But Sally, if there had been no Tiny Tim then we wouldn't have a word to describe all those disabled people who sell out and reinforce negative stereotypical portraits of disabled people.

At which point Malcolm added the footnote

A few years after the Carol had come out, the Tiny Tim Guild was created, a charitable trust to look after the crippled children of England.

And this teed up Mike Oliver's final say: 'And I bet it was run by able-bodied people!'

The historical view

Perhaps the fear and dread of disability, fleshed out by Dickens and so many other writers, can be traced back to something very primeval. By the law of the wild the ill, the injured and the disabled fall by the wayside. It is supposedly part of natural selection. The sickly wildebeest calf dropped by its mother on the African plain is quickly devoured by the hyenas. In small primitive tribal groups the disabled person may have been seen as a liability. Certainly this century the Nazis referred to disabled people as the 'useless eaters' and thus justified the condemnation and despatch of many hundreds of thousands of disabled people to the gas chambers.

There are many societies where the disabled person is nurtured and often seen as a source of wisdom or particular skill. There is evidence to suggest that the Olmecs of ancient Mexico regarded people with Down's Syndrome as divine visitors and made statues and figurines of them.

Yet the harsher view of disability appears to have been more common in history. The ancient Athenians left disabled children in the open air, to die of starvation or to be taken by wolves or foxes. It was quite legal and acceptable to practise this deliberate neglect. The purpose in those days may well have been economic, but it probably also contained an element of the concept of eugenics, later enthusiastically embraced by the Nazis.

A similar train of thought can be seen in Christian history. In his book *Mental Handicap... Is Anything Wrong?*, David Potter refers to a story about Martin Luther, who is accused by historians of teaching that people with mental handicaps have no soul and should be drowned. David Potter questions the source of the story but does not consider it wholly inconsistent with the culture of Luther's day.

Luther is reputed to have told his friends the story of a tussle he had with a twelve-year-old boy in Dessau. The boy was apparently mentally handicapped and behaved in a disgusting manner. Luther is said to have advised the Prince of Anhalt: 'If I were the Prince, I should take this child to the Moldau River which flows near Dessau and drown him.' The advice was refused. He then suggested: 'Well then, the Christians shall order the Lord's Prayer to be said in church and pray that the dear Lord take the Devil away.' This was done daily in Dessau and the 'changeling' died in the following year.

The incident bears closer examination in two respects. First, we need to understand the way mental handicap was commonly understood in his day. A child with a deformity or mental handicap was said to be not the baby as it was born to its mother, but a replacement left by fairies or demons. This view was adapted from pagan folklore and Christianized. Explanations for this strange exchange were that the parents were guilty of some wickedness, or that the parents loved the

child more than they loved God, or that the mother had been
seduced by the devil. If Luther should reflect in some respects
the religious culture of his day we should not be surprised.

The unashamed eugenics practised centuries later by the Nazis was
justified by the nightmarish proposition that society should consist solely of
physically perfect people and that selected breeding and culling—birth
control and euthanasia—need to be adopted to achieve that end. This
approach may be acceptable when restricted to the breeding of prize cats
or farm animals, but when applied to human beings it appears not only
callous but horrendous in its implications. Yet even now, after the deeds of
the Nazis have been made public, eugenics still exists. It could even be said
that today it is pursued equally diligently but under a different guise, and that
the aborting of genetically deformed foetuses and the attempts by scientists
to eradicate certain types of genes have the same purpose.

The Romans, however, realized that disabled people could have a value
as a source of entertainment, and mocking disabled people, particularly
those with learning disabilities, has been common all the way through to
this century. In Britain Bethlehem Hospital in London—or Bedlam, to give
it its colloquial name—provided Sunday afternoon entertainment for many
decades. The public flocked to view the 'lunatics' in the madhouse, many
of whom, if classified today, would be generally described as having mental
handicaps or mental disabilities, although some would also be labelled
more specifically with a syndrome to describe a collection of symptoms
resulting from a common cause.

Some disabled people have turned the mocking of disability back
onto the mockers. Steady Eddy, an Australian stand-up comic who has
cerebral palsy, disturbed the peace of mind of many by coming out with
bad-taste jokes aimed at himself.

At one point in his act he would look at the audience and say 'I've
come to the conclusion it's me who's normal. Why else would so
many of you, after a forty-hour week go to the pub and down twenty
schooners just so as to walk like me?' He also turned a neat line in
referring to his days at a special school in Australia. 'My teachers said
we should be inconspicuous and blend in with society, so they sent a
bus to pick me up from home every day with Spastic Centre written
on the side. Inconspicuous, eh?'

His approach, it should be pointed out, has been roundly criticized by other disabled comedians. The British stand-up comedienne Wanda Barbara accused him of making it legitimate to laugh at disabled people and to make 'spastic jokes'. She said his act helped reinforce stereotypes, not challenge them. While she empathized with his line about the Spastic Centre bus, she would rule out all jokes in which he mocked himself.

Instead, she turns such humour on its head. In one of her stories she tells of being in a supermarket with one of her young children. Suddenly the child asks, 'Why is that man walking in a straight line?' 'Ssh,' she says, embarrassed by the question—and then whispers, 'He's able-bodied.'

The singer/songwriter Simon Smith, who says that disability politics is part of his life, uses savage language in his songs to shock and mock the mainstream world.

On 'Does He Take Sugar?' in December 1993 he said, 'Some people think I've got a chip on my shoulder the size of a sixty-two-storey tower block while to other people I'm not political enough.'

This one couplet from a song should give a feel as to what his work is about:

Oppression—it's alive and well.
The black man's still in chains while the cripple rings a bell.

Much of the savage irony of his work is summed up in the title of his supporting group: 'The Useless Eaters'.

We tried to reclaim some language which the Nazis used: it was a term they used for disabled people, 'the useless eaters'. Part of the reason for using that expression was because contemporary society still has feelings regarding disability which relate to Nazi ideas. It partly goes to eugenics, the creation of perfect people and so there's the idea of getting rid of disabled people through abortions and genetic engineering. It's trying to make a statement about that and bring up the issue.

Is Simon seriously saying we are going back to that era and way of thinking?

In Germany at the moment there's been over seventy attacks on disabled people in the last year; only yesterday there were attacks made on old disabled people in Britain. I feel that people's concern about disability at the moment is negligible. They only like to use them to make themselves feel better when it comes to charity events.

Part of the reason for doing the album is to get people to be aware that having a disability isn't the end of life. In fact life can be even richer for having a disability. So if you look at the lyrics, if you hear the lyrics in the song you'll find that most of the points made are quite logical, concise, you know they're not just emotionally backed arguments, they're actually trying to make relevant points to the able-bodied people as well.

In one song Simon writes,

You don't need a bunch of Nazis
when you've got misinformed political parties.

That line originally comes from the fact that a few years ago legislation regarding abortions and disabled people was changed. My feelings concerning political parties and disability issues is that they have very little understanding of the reality of disability. You get like the Chancellor the other day, talking about invalids. He hasn't even got any idea of politically correct language, so why these people should actually be making decisions regarding our life is beyond me.

Yet will Simon's songs and other art by people with disabilities for people with disabilities reach out to the wider world?

We specifically wrote some of the songs regarding disability to be for an able-bodied audience and we're trying to get them to understand the issues and so far our experience has been that most people are very interested by the lyrics.

People who are born with disabilities are very much shaped by their experience of life. Would Simon have been a very different person in character and outlook if he had been born with the lower parts of his two arms?

I think you can't deny that if you've got a disability it permeates your whole personality, because of how people react to you. I expect around the age of two or something like that, one becomes aware that one's different and is affected by that. Also how you're actually treated, what happens to you, whether your parents keep you. A lot of disabled people are abandoned because they don't fit in with the culturally accepted child, so that kind of thing can have a big effect on your life as well.

These days that abandonment may not be to the forces of nature on a hillside but to the local social services, who are then obliged to keep the child in care or advertise for foster parents. It is undoubtedly the case that a very high proportion of children seeking foster or adoptive parents have disabilities.

What will historians of the future make of the cultures, secular and religious, of today as they examine the subject of disability? It is perhaps here that a distinction needs to be made between those disabilities which have resulted from a genetic cause or have their root in a birth or prenatal trauma, and those which have been caused by a subsequent accident or disease after the individual concerned has known a period of life without the disability. It is a distinction which is important, notwithstanding the point, which cannot be emphasized enough, that every individual's experience of disability is unique.

4

THE VALUE OF LIFE

Is all human life valuable? Or are there categories of value which make a difference in the way people with different disabilities are treated in society and how they regard themselves? Certainly, different issues are brought up by, for example, a division into people who have disabilities from birth and others who are disabled later in life.

Birth disability

Parents who produce a disabled child go through agonies of guilt and resentment, often with little support, having had their anxieties compounded by embarrassed medical staff who broach the subject in a crass and insensitive way. Often the professionals make assumptions about how the parents will react and compound the problem by delaying the news. A report produced by SCOPE (then still named the Spastics Society) entitled *Right From the Start* and published in 1994 described ways in which parents were told about their child's disability.

The report talked of the anger and distress of parents who had been kept in ignorance. Sometimes they felt their emotions had been manipulated, that an assumption had been made that the mother might reject her child and that the longer the news was delayed the better the chance of bonding.

In one case, the mother complained that the medical assessment of her daughter had been so badly handled that it was not until her child was nearly two that she realized she had special needs.

Although I knew my daughter had problems, cerebral palsy was never mentioned until she was nearly two. The consultant labelled my daughter and didn't bother to explain anything to me. As you can imagine, I only know the worst from what I have seen in the media and was most distressed and wondered what all the hard work my husband and I had put in to teach our daughter to crawl was for, if she was going to end up in a wheelchair.

In another case a parent described how her son Davie was seen at a special baby unit at the age of eleven months where a consultant, while not saying what was wrong, agreed that the baby's motor control was not developing as it should and arranged for him to have some home visits by a specially trained worker.

When the trained worker arrived at the home she asked about Davie and about his hearing and about his sleep. Janet, Davie's mother, said that his sleep was dreadful.

'Oh, that's very common with children with cerebral palsy,' she replied. I nearly fell off the settee, it was the first time I had heard cerebral palsy mentioned and that's how we heard.

The helper had heard the diagnosis from the clinic and thought that Janet knew.

The report concluded:

Parents often have to struggle against other people's attitudes... they also describe their distress and depression, the complexity of their responses, above all, their sense of isolation. All the more reason that the reactions of other people should play a part in solving, and not be allowed to be part of, their problems. Other writers have pointed out the dangers in the 'medical' or the 'tragic' approach to disability. In respect to diagnosis and disclosure, those dangers are no less real than they are at any other stage of the life of someone with a disability.

Everyone with children has 'offered hostages to fortune'. It may well be that this inherent vulnerability of all parents is one of the factors that complicates the social response to the birth of a disabled child.

A tiny proportion of children (only 3 per cent) are born with a disability. In the not so distant past, such an event was usually seen as a tragic manifestation of divine retribution for the sins of the parents. Even very recently, 'master race' myths, and misguided notions of human perfectibility, have been used to justify the exclusion of people with disabilities from the mainstream of life, or even from life itself.

But our society, on the whole, is struggling towards the civilized view that all people share equal value as human beings, and that the extent to which that concept is realized in practice is a measure of the stature of any society.

The practice of parenting

In 1994 I visited Belfast to talk to a group of mothers whose children had been born with multiple and profound disabilities. They were members of SENSE Northern Ireland, and had come together to offer each other mutual support. Each had found the experience of being the mother of a profoundly disabled child a difficult and isolating experience.

I have visited Northern Ireland many times as a news reporter and correspondent, but I do not think I have ever returned from the province with quite so much to sort out in my own mind as from that visit. It had nothing to do with the Troubles except, perhaps, that the people I met, Protestant and Catholic alike, had much to teach the politicians. As members of the charity SENSE Northern Ireland they formed a self-help and support group for parents of children with profound (and I mean profound) disabilities. Ann McManus, a Protestant—although in this context such labelling is barely relevant—told me about her ten-year-old daughter Jill, who has a rare and multiply disabling syndrome.

She's blind, she's partially deaf, she has no language, she has learning difficulties and she's facially deformed. She has one eye missing, one ear missing and she has a peculiar bone in her spine but the problems didn't really start until she lost the sight of her remaining eye. She also had a cleft palate and after it was repaired she then lost part of her hearing. She's a very happy child most of the time; she's very active; thankfully, she knows exactly what she wants now, thanks to a lot of input and advice she can get her message over very well. I would say I'm probably one of the luckier ones.

Most of the children for whom SENSE now exists were born with profound disabilities. A generation ago many would not have survived the first few days although as Maria Prigent, a Catholic, told me, her six-year-old daughter Ashling was born with problems which suddenly and dramatically worsened.

Ashling was born with a renal problem and deaf, but other than that she would have been mentally okay. She'd have been running about and all that. I just can't accept that it was all taken away from her at seven months. She went to bed practically a normal healthy child and we found her the next morning just the way she has been from then on. So I'll never accept the way she is. I mean I still live in hope that something's going to come back, if it was taken away from her overnight. I'm living in hope that through time maybe her sight will come back. I think the future's going to be very hard for Ashling. If you don't lift her and do things with her Ashling would just be left to lie there, she depends on other people and without SENSE and with the future they're trying to build for the children—they're trying to build day centres, resource centres and eventually, residential care, and they will have the staff and the equipment there that will provide the necessary input and stimulation for these children—without that Ashling wouldn't have much of a future at all.

SENSE Northern Ireland started life in 1984 after one of the founding parents, Muriel Mathers, had seen a television documentary about SENSE on the UK mainland. Her daughter Sarah is now fifteen but Muriel's recollections of the early days are still vivid. Sarah had been born with the multiple disabilities associated with rubella.

My father hadn't seen Sarah in hospital. She was in the intensive care unit and we took him up and while we were holding Sarah up to let him have a look the sister came over and she said to me, 'Oh, by the way, we've just discovered she's got a hole in the heart, okay?' And I looked at my husband and I said to him, 'If you don't get me out of here I will wreck this place.' And the sister then said, 'Oh, perhaps I didn't tell you in the right way.' And I said, 'No, Sister, I'm sorry, you did not tell me in the right way.'

When Muriel returned home the professionals were equally flat-footed.

The district nurse called to see Sarah and I explained Sarah was still in hospital, she'd had a few problems. The nurse asked what exactly was wrong with the baby. So I explained to her briefly the few problems that Sarah had and the nurse said to me, 'Well, what have you bought for this child?' I said, 'Just the usual vests, nappies.' And the nurse replied, 'Don't waste too much money; this child isn't going to live anyway.' She was one of the old brigade, just blunt and to the point.

Frances Tolland joined SENSE last December. The life of her daughter Marie Louise has also more than once hung by a thread.

She's now three and a half years old. I had no support for her for the first two years of her life because nobody could tell me what to look for or what to be doing with her. It was just a fortnightly visit to the hospital for half hour's physio, because she's quite floppy; she doesn't feed, she's fed through a tube straight into her stomach. She's a very pleasant child; she's had a lot of problems, she's coped with them all. I mean she's had to battle her three and a half years. When she's ill she can be quite cross, when she's well she's a very pleasant child.

And had Frances been told how long the doctors expected Marie Louise to live?

No. When I think she's doing pretty well and I am so proud of the tiny wee things that she's managing to do, I mean she loves to lie on the floor happily and she'll move one arm and one leg spontaneously and I'll be delighted with her doing this. She knows how to laugh and how to cry and for a while we knew she could even feel pain. I went to see her consultants to ask about what she would be able to do. They painted her future very black and I think they are completely baffled that she's lived this long and is doing relatively well.

When the time comes for Marie Louise to go to school, Frances will have the experience of other parents to draw on. Muriel Mathers was on her own when Sarah came of school age. After many rebuffs she found one school, in West Belfast, which would take her. To get Sarah there Muriel had to drive up the Catholic Falls Road, a thing very few people from out of the area would have dared do.

That school was a little haven of peace in all of this turmoil. The headmistress was a nun. I am a Protestant. She was a beautiful person. I went up and down there four times a day for eight years through IRA bomb scares, gun battles; you name it, we were up there and if it hadn't been for that nun I honestly don't think I would be here today.

Nobody else wanted Sarah, but the sister could see that I needed help and she said to me, 'No matter what the authorities say, you bring Sarah up and we'll help you,' and she did. And that was a beautiful relationship which lasted eight years.

Up until 1991 there was no record in the province of the total number of people who were deaf and blind. When Margaret Dodds joined SENSE as full-time development officer in 1990 she set to with the government agencies to compile the figures.

We discovered from the survey that there were 480 people who had a dual-sensory disability, quite substantial and then of those 114 were children. We then discovered that a third of those people had severe mobility difficulties and around a third again had severe communication problems. The main way I think that SENSE can help the parents is really by giving them support in the early stages. Then we can offer specialized advice and information and offer assessments. We'd be looking at what residual sight and hearing they have and also how we can help that child who is developmentally delayed to progress.

SENSE now provides a place on the outskirts of Belfast which not only has specialist equipment for the children but also gives parents a place to meet. Parents of children with similar disabilities give advice to each other and share experiences, maybe just practical things about how to improve feeding or stop a child from choking, or loosen up their limbs. All parents know that, whatever the back-up, progress is only achieved with patience and perseverance. Frances Tolland explained:

You practically watch every blink of their eyes or every movement; when Marie Louise makes a move with her little face you try and work on it and try and expand it and encourage it to come on. I don't know why she ever started smiling, she just did and then we started tickling her and finding all these tickly spots. You would think somebody had given me a million pounds, I'm so delighted with those moments. When Marie Louise just laughs or she gives you a knowing look, or whenever she starts to respond to different things that you are doing with her, nothing else in the world could ever replace that for you. It just makes you feel so good inside and it takes away some of that hurt that is always buried somewhere inside you.

And SENSE's accumulating specialist knowledge helps parents solve what seem like intractable problems. Ann McManus couldn't get her daughter to take anything but liquid food.

Jill was what they called tactilely defensive; she wouldn't tolerate certain textures, she wouldn't tolerate lumpy food. We began by mixing up a box of peas, lentils, rice, pasta, that sort of thing and rubbing it over the back of her hands then over her legs, moving up her body until she tolerated it. Once she knew that there were lumpy things in life, well then it was easier to teach her to eat lumpy food. She never went through what they call a finger feeding phase because she was tactilely defensive. She wouldn't touch the food, but once she could feel it with her fingers then she accepted it.

Today Jill lives with her mother at home, though even a generation ago she would have probably been put away in a home.

Most definitely, and I expect with her facial deformities she may have been pushed into an attic and forgotten about. I mean thirty to forty years ago I'm sure there weren't too many people like Jill wandering around.

I would now not be without her; after ten years of thinking and feeling and generally loving in such a close proximity with the child I cannot see myself without her, I don't remember life without her.

I can now cope with the public reaction to her, what people say and what people do. I've taught myself to deal with it. The normal reaction is for people to stare. They stare. Children quite often follow me. I've been in supermarkets where sometimes I've ended up with as many as seven children. I feel a bit like the Pied Piper sometimes. I don't like to knock other people with normal children because I'm quite sure if I had normal children I would be very proud of them and look forward to twenty-first birthdays and weddings and grandchildren and all the rest. Sometimes I sit back and I think about what I'm not going to have, what I'm going to miss out on and how some day I probably won't be able to cope with Jill and our home will not be enough for her. She will have to go somewhere that will fulfil her needs then. While other people's children go off and get married it will not be the same for me, when I give up my daughter she'll be lost to me.

69

Ann admits Jill does not know what she's missing in life, but she, as her mother, hurts for her. Yet why make so much effort to help children who'll only achieve so very little? A difficult question I put to Margaret Dodds.

These children have a right to the best in life as all our children have a right. Sometimes people say 'Well, why bother?' But you can see progression and you can see multi-disabled children being helped and enabled. Who knows how many of these children will progress to even greater things? With disability it is not always static and I feel personally that with many of these children, with the right sort of help and appropriate specialized support, they can progress and they will progress.

But there is always the pain underneath, as Murial Mathers admitted.

When you have a handicapped child, to me it is a continuing sense of bereavement. Every day of my life there's a sense of loss. When Sarah goes on the bus, all the children wave bye-bye except my own daughter. She doesn't recognize me. She's fifteen now and I remember when I was fifteen the things I did. Basically she's a baby, yet you can't dress her in frilly clothes. It just goes on and on and it's just a continual sense of loss of what might have been.

And then come the agonizing decisions. When a profoundly disabled child is offered medical treatment, should the child be put through the trauma of surgery and suffering? Is it worth it? Muriel's Sarah, for instance, has a heart condition. The surgeons say an operation might help. Should she have it?

It is a no win situation. I hope the decision is taken out of my hands. If the time arrives when she needs the operation and I say no, I will feel that I will have condemned my daughter to death. If I put her through the operation and she dies in the operating theatre I have lost again. If she survives, her quality of life is such that I will ask myself, do I really want her to be left

70

the way she is? If there is a God I would hope that in his infinite
mercy he would solve the problem for me and that Sarah would
die a natural death. I just wouldn't want her to suffer any more.

Every parent of a profoundly disabled child must face that dilemma.
Is my child's life really worth fighting for? Would it not be easier if he or
she died a peaceful, natural death? Today of course those questions can
be faced at a much earlier stage. Parents can be offered the possibility
of that child never being allowed to develop fully in the womb and not
being born.

Should they be born?

It is now almost standard practice in countries with advanced scientific
medical facilities, at least in those cases where there is believed to be a
high risk of inherited disability, for a pregnant mother to be offered an
amniocentesis by her doctor. This is a procedure whereby a test
sample of the amniotic, or womb fluid, is taken and analyzed. The fluid
will give the laboratory information about possible congenital
abnormalities in the foetus.

Should any problem be spotted, the mother is offered a termination
of that pregnancy. This is an area of ethics which causes considerable
concern to many Christians who are otherwise totally opposed to
abortions. Might there not be some occasions, if severe disabilities are
diagnosed which would result in the child having a limited and
seemingly purposeless life, for that life to be brought to a premature
end? Naturally having the test and being required to react to its results
is a time of great anxiety for parents. Some parents will be in no doubt
that it is the right thing to end the pregnancy. Others will hope and pray
the pregnancy naturally aborts and they will not be faced with an
ultimate and irrevocable decision. Yet a third group will know that
whatever difficulties might allow they cannot in all conscience consent
to an abortion.

In that these medical possibilities now exist, the questions posed are
not confined to potential parents. If the foetus cannot express a view,
other disabled people now living, who might have been candidates for

abortions, can speak out. What are the messages they are getting from this medical and ethical debate? It could be argued that the messages are not dissimilar to those given out by Martin Luther all those centuries ago.

A few years ago I visited a centre near Ilkely in Yorkshire where young people born with spina bifida and hydrocephalus were learning the skills of independent living. At the time of writing the centre's future is uncertain. These young people in their twenties and thirties were a special generation, for if they had been any older, medical science could not have saved their lives, or at least could not have given them the chance of living anything approaching their present life, and yet if they had been conceived much later their parents might well have accepted the choice of an abortion.

In our conversation it became quite evident that they had considered the implications of this debate, and had more right than most to offer a view. However there was no common voice. It is hard to realize that one is the sort of person even one's parents might be wishing had never been born. To some it is a devastating realization. Others contemplating the question conclude it might have been better if they had never been brought into this world, they have endured so difficult and painful a life, and part of that pain inevitably has been the knowledge that one is not deemed to be a fit person to live.

Of course, no one says these things in so many words, and I have no reason to suppose the young people I met do not have, in the main, loving friends and families. I am talking about implied impressions coming at them from society at large. The message comes through clearly in day to day contact, reading the newspapers, watching television drama or listening to moral debates on the radio. When a pundit muses over the question: should mothers known to be carrying a 'malformed' foetus be allowed an abortion? there are always disabled listeners who know that pundit is talking about them.

Disability in later life

The questions highlighted by the experiences of the people I met at Ilkely are very different from those which would be posed by others who had been disabled later in life. While they share some of the 'Why has it happened and why to me?' questions, many also ask of themselves how they were to blame for their disability or how they should cope with the guilt of others who may have been responsible. A person injured by a terrorist bomb will nurture anger and may find it impossible, or at least very difficult, to contemplate Christian forgiveness. Turning the other cheek is all very well, but do you offer the other leg to be mutilated by the terrorist?

Few people have the astonishing depth of faith and calm courage of Gordon Wilson, the father of Marie killed by terrorists at Enniskillen in 1987, who went on to become a respected peace campaigner until his own death in 1995.

The wall collapsed... and we were thrown forward... rubble and stones... all around us and under us. I remember thinking... 'I'm not hurt'... but there's a pain in my shoulder... I shouted to Marie, 'Are you all right?' and she said 'Yes'... She found my hand and said, 'Is that your hand, Dad?'... I said, 'Are you all right, dear?'... but we were under six feet of rubble... three or four times I asked her... she always said, 'Yes, I'm all right'... I asked her the fifth time... 'Are you all right, Marie?'... She said, 'Daddy, I love you very much...' Those were the last words she spoke to me... I kept shouting, 'Marie, are you all right?'... There was no reply... I have lost my daughter, but I bear no ill will, I bear no grudge... Dirty sort of talk is not going to bring her back to life... I don't have an answer... But I know there has to be a plan. If I didn't think that, I would commit suicide... It's part of a greater plan, and God is good... And we shall meet again.

And then there is the anguish of the husband badly injured in a motor accident in which he has been driving, for which he is to blame, and in which also one of his children has been killed. He will undergo agonizing guilt. Some of the people with the most difficult task are those injured in war. After some wars the victors return as heroes, but this is unusual. More often the injured serviceman returns to his family as a stranger and to a nation which is indifferent to his 'sacrifice'. This indifference was particularly evident in the USA after the Vietnam war.

The nation felt too guilty or even too embarrassed to acknowledge the war-wounded.

At the same time as coping with both psychological and physical pain, most disabled people will come face to face with indignities of disability which have been imposed from society. In 1985 Lois Keith, a mother of two young daughters and a part-time educational researcher, was hit by a speeding motorist and paralyzed from the chest down.

Nine years on, in an introduction to a collection of essays and poems by disabled women, *Mustn't Grumble*, she wrote this:

After my accident, I found that the beliefs which we had always shared about equality and justice were not enough to help me understand the complicated and sometimes hostile world in which I now found myself as a disabled person...

I began to understand that my inability to be a full part of this society was not, in fact, my fault. Important things were made inaccessible to me, not because of my inability to walk, but because of laws and regulations which were designed to shut me out. I was now living in a society which had permission to exclude me from things I had grown to consider my right, like access to public buildings, employment, or just being able to go to the cinema of my choice on a Saturday night. I had now become someone people felt sorry for, someone who could be approached by total strangers in public places and asked intrusive questions...

Later, when I learnt that life was going to be good after all, I began to try to make sense of the society I live in, the prejudice and fear of disability, the encounters with strangers that unsettled and disturbed me, and the images of myself I met through books I had grown up with. I was concerned, too, with the current popular debate about the rights and needs of those who 'cared for' disabled people, which somehow left me out altogether. Where was my position in this world as a disabled woman, how was I to make sense of it all and come through it, confident and strong?

People who use wheelchairs, but are otherwise coherent and outwardly personable, suffer far less by way of prejudice than people with communication problems or learning difficulties. When it comes to issues of civil rights no one would suggest that a lively young articulate wheelchair user should be disenfranchised, although it is the case that many polling stations are inaccessible. Nor would anyone suggest that such a person should not get married. Yet the assumption is made, on behalf of many other disabled people, that they would not be capable of performing any civil duties or of taking on any domestic ties.

Frequently disabled people of 'lower status' report considerable intrusion from family and caring professionals into their private lives. In particular the outside world feels free to intrude in matters of personal and sexual relations.

Michelle Mason is the mother of a daughter who shares her disability. Both have a syndrome which involves restricted physical growth, restricted mobility and a very distinct set of facial characteristics. In no way is Michelle mentally disabled, yet, as a child she recalls how her potential future as a parent was never raised. She discussed such matters with her peers, but not with teachers or carers. 'It was our own secret world,' she recalls. It seemed to her that as she was disabled everyone else assumed that she had no sexuality.

Mental illness: unacceptable disability

Mental illness is also frequently very socially disabling. Not only does it still have a stigma attached to it but mental health problems can often make it difficult to cope with the everyday decisions and responsibilities of living. It is a sad fact that hundreds of people with a history of mental illness end up as homeless. Two years ago a report was produced by the Richmond Fellowship together with the Glasgow Council for Single Homeless and some of the cases highlighted made disturbing reading.

From the evidence of campaign workers and other support workers, a picture emerged of a steady rise in the number of mentally ill people who were becoming homeless. They seemed to be being discharged directly from hospital into the community; not just long-stay patients but the majority of younger mentally ill people were ending up in the homeless hostels without any support, quite often being discharged from one agency into another, a scenario known as the revolving door syndrome. Young people were being sent to and from area teams, accident and emergency wards, general hospitals, acute admission wards, prisons and police stations without any co-ordinated agency response. The situation, it was feared, was destined to get worse. Two thousand patients were expected to be discharged in Glasgow over five years. The question raised by the report was, will there be the choices of accommodation and will there be the support?

I met Jacqueline Munro who lived in one of the city's hostels for single homeless; she now has a room of her own with communal facilities and her illness is kept stable by regular medication.

On and off I've been ill since I was about fourteen, I would say fourteen years old. I've been in the psychiatric hospitals you know.

I was hearing voices, I was suicidal, I was psychotic, manic, I mean the whole lot.

Now the condition is under control because of medication and I really want to give it a try this time and really succeed and live a normal life.

So what sort of help and back-up does Jacqueline need to achieve this?

It's difficult to say, because I was semi-evicted from my house for damages and rent arrears and the psychiatrist and social workers' council had a meeting to see if I would get my house back. I was pregnant at the time, but they decided they should evict me and they left me staying with someone who was violent towards me and they discharged me from hospital when I was ill. I was not fully recovered but I've pulled through quite a lot so I'm staying in the hostel now and I hope maybe a psychiatrist can get me somewhere sheltered accommodation.

Any return to a settled life depends on the regular medication.

*In the past I've failed to take the injections. I've been in prison
as well and when I was in prison I wouldn't take it for the nine
months I was there. I was sort of psychotic and if I didn't take
this injection I would probably end up back in hospital again or
end up doing something silly, attempted suicide or whatever.*

There is however another scenario, that of the long-term patients
leaving institutions who end up as homeless. Jimmy Lang was fifty years
in, as he puts it, 'the system', confined first as a hyperactive child. Now
married and living a fully independent life, he stays very much aware of
the difficulties of adjusting to the outside world. He tells this story of a
man he saw sitting by himself in Glasgow city centre.

*He was sitting with a spoon and a plate and institution was
there, the hall mark. I sat down, we spoke away and I says, 'You
don't mind me asking you, have you ever been in a psychiatric
hospital?' and his reply was, 'Oh aye, son, twenty-two years, but
the doctor thought I was ready to look after myself.' Now there
was he sleeping in George's Square. How dare they! It is a
complete and utter negation of duty and that's it in a nutshell.*

There is no Glasgow cardboard city but nevertheless the council has
only a limited range of options when someone presents themselves as
homeless. The majority of people end up in one of the large hostels,
because that is, in the short term, the only or the quickest route to
putting a roof over their head. For many people who get into the hostel
system it is not appropriate accommodation. There are other options;
a variety of furnished flats are available, but in terms of numbers and in
terms of immediate response, large numbers of homeless mentally ill
people do end up in the hostels, council or private.

The hostels provide basic accommodation and the staff in them, while
they are skilled and caring, are not trained or equipped to provide the
whole range of support services for people with mental health problems.

In London the situation is far worse. Now it is so common for
ordinary people going about their business to see a mentally ill person
shouting, ranting or just huddled and shivering in an office doorway,
that it barely rates any note.

While medication might seem the key to the problem, and drugs exist to suppress the disturbing symptoms of mental illness, many people disabled by a psychiatric condition are reluctant to take medication on a regular basis. The medication, they feel, dulls their sensitivities and turns them into doped, compliant vegetables. This reluctance to turn to medication is particularly strong when an individual patient suffers from some form of cyclical condition. They note that for most of the time life can be enjoyed without these powerful drugs and it is only at times of crisis that they need help. They resent being required by doctors to suppress their normal lives in order to fend off crises. Their call is for the availability of crisis centres to which they can go when their delusions and anxieties overwhelm them.

Recent cases reported in newspapers, such as two involving men who climbed into the lions' cage at London Zoo, have worried the politicians, who now favour introducing legal ways by which psychiatric patients can be compelled to take prescribed medication.

Does the church care?

Apart from the medical and caring professions, who can a parent or a disabled person turn to at a time of need? Obviously close family play an important part, but who else is there to provide neutral support and understanding? Is it a fitting role for the church and if so, as it must surely be, how well equipped are priests, ministers and congregations?

In the same way that medical students are taught to recognize rare diseases but given little insight into a day to day understanding of disability, so the clergy are trained in biblical criticism and to recognize a range of theological nuance, but seldom get the chance to learn how to communicate with a disabled person seeking for answers. True, how can one train for such circumstances? Experience is what counts, but an awareness of the problems can be passed on.

When a disabled person wants to make contact it is often very difficult to make a contact at sufficient depth and in a way that is helpful. The first reaction of some Christians is that the disabled person should seek wholeness through faith, implying this necessary wholeness is physical as well as spiritual.

A Roman Catholic may be encouraged to take a pilgrimage to Lourdes, and while no one is told they will experience a physical miracle, the expectation is in the air. The piles of discarded crutches near the shrine give a powerful message. Similarly, a Protestant may be encouraged to go and hear a preacher with a healing ministry. A huge crowd will be whipped into religious fervour. Expectations will be raised. One well-known preacher was severely criticized recently for a poster campaign in which he implied that miracle healings were there for the asking. Some unscrupulous preachers have resorted to knavish tricks.

There is the wheelchair scam for instance. In one case I was told about, a vulnerable person entered the hall, walking but in some pain. A steward asked if they wished to be prayed over. The individual had arthritis and indeed wished to have relief from the pain. She was shown to the front of the hall by the steward, who reassured her that in the front row the preacher would be bound to see her. The only seat left in the front row was an empty wheelchair. 'You don't mind sitting there just for a while, until they get another chair?'

However the other chair never arrived and before long the lights dimmed, the preacher entered and the razzmatazz was underway. The arthritic woman forgot she was in a wheelchair and was caught up in the excitement of the moment. In due course the preacher came to her.

'Do you wish to be healed?' said the preacher.

'Yes,' the woman replied, hoping for some relief from the discomfort of her condition.

'Then, in the name of Jesus, stand,' the preacher commanded.

She stood.

'Walk towards me,' said the preacher.

The woman obeyed. There was a gasp of astonishment from the audience: a woman in a wheelchair had stood and walked. They had witnessed a miracle. The woman concerned was too embarrassed to say anything once she realized what had happened. She later left the hall disillusioned and in the same pain, but everyone who had seen her marvelled at her miraculous recovery.

Such deliberate fraudulent activity is rare. More common is over-exaggeration in claiming healings at such rallies, a failure to follow up superficial success and a raising of fake hope. In Roman Catholic circles there can be an overemphasis on the almost magical properties of relics.

It would be wrong to paint an entirely negative picture of the church's healing ministry. For although it can be argued that miraculous physical healings are very unusual, the healing ministry has a much wider purpose. Frequently it simply allows people to know that the church understands. Many people derive comfort from the laying on of hands and are helped by being embraced by the love of the church in this way. They do not expect to walk out of the healing service leaping where once they could only totter, but they do feel a sense of healing through the church's support.

Pilgrims to Lourdes tell stories of healings, yet very seldom do they revolve around miraculous physical intervention. Indeed attested miracles, investigated and accepted by the Roman Catholic church, are very rare. What pilgrims talk about frequently is how their own feelings of bitterness and resentment towards their disabilities are eased by visiting the famous shrine. Sometimes this comes about simply by seeing others who appear to accept or cope with even more crippling conditions than their own with good cheer. Other pilgrims find that the periods of prayer and meditation or the uplifting ceremonial benefits the spirit and thus enables them to carry a physical burden in life with greater ease.

Another response of a well-motivated church friend to a disability in another might be that of over-protectiveness. At every opportunity that friend offers to help, so much so that he or she becomes a nuisance to the disabled person. The disabled person yearns for space and not to be the constant focus of care, attention and pity, but the do-gooding friend probably has little understanding of what is going on—he or she may well get a buzz from doing good works and being seen to do so. Finding the right balance between helping and intruding is difficult, and there is little theological guidance on this very practical subject.

5

THE POWER DEFICIT

Disabled people frequently find themselves in a position of powerlessness, whether it is lack of financial resources, lack of political goodwill or lack of acceptance as full human beings. This power deficit can be redressed, but it must be done by the powerful accepting their claims to power-sharing as just, something that does not have many historical precedents.

Frequently the most disabling thing about being disabled is being poor. For many reasons, including a widespread prejudice about employing people with disabilities, disabled people rely upon the benefits system for an income. In Britain the benefits system is far from generous and is organized in such a way that any individual entitled to a benefit is made to struggle to get it.

The benefits maze

Claims forms are complex and to get a benefit often requires many visits to offices and professionals. There is the feeling that everything is given with a grudge. There are also many petty regulations which make life unnecessarily difficult.

One good example of this came to light in May 1993. A new updated and revised list of items attracting VAT was published by Customs and Excise. Disabled people suddenly found they were paying 17.5 per cent extra, in the form of tax, on a range of items including such things as cushioned toilet seats, adjustable leg rests, a type of small bed pad, a style of folding walking stick and adjustable over-bed tables. It was argued by Customs and Excise that by law the only items justifiably exempt from VAT were those which were solely made for and used by disabled people.

In one particular case which was taken to appeal, an electronic nerve stimulator specifically designed for and used by people suffering chronic pain was taxed because, said the Paymaster General, some sportsmen and -women were believed to make use of it when they were injured.

While some disabled people could reclaim the VAT the procedures were time-consuming and arbitrary.

And then there are the curious anomalies in the tightly worded regulations. The section 37 (Z) (C) of the 1975 Social Security Act, as amended by the Disability Living Allowance and Disability Working Allowance Act 1991, prevents children receiving the mobility component of the Disability Living Allowance until they are five years old. In one case highlighted involving triplets, two of whom had cerebral palsy and obvious and acute walking difficulties, the regulations prevented their mother from receiving any extra help until the children's fifth birthday even though from an early age the difficulties and expenses involved in transporting them around were every bit as great as they would have been after their fifth birthday.

And arbitrary rules and penny-pinching is not confined to central government. In 1993 Staffordshire County Council set out its regulations for what it described as handicapped person's holidays. The County Council offered to provide an escort to accompany disabled people to the holiday camp at Weston-super-Mare which had been booked. The escort would be someone listed as a recognized county escort, to be allocated by a special services officer. A special point, however, was made in the regulations that the council would not pay for any escort 'belonging to the same family as the handicapped person'.

In another clause it said that to qualify for the holiday the disabled person must not be going on holiday elsewhere in the same year and 'if it is discovered that you have had or are to have another holiday you will immediately be withdrawn from this holiday and you may be in danger of forfeiting any monies you have paid'.

Amongst other points noted by Staffordshire in making their amazing holiday offer was that some types of wheelchairs would not be able to go through some of the bathroom doorways (even if doors are taken off) and that special diets could not be catered for.

Of course it is easy to point out absurdities in a system with a turnover of billions of pounds a year. Anomalies are bound to occur. But the overwhelming impression articulated by disabled people on benefit is that the benefit always falls short of requirements, appears to be kept as tight as possible and that life with a disability is made that much more of a struggle by financial worries.

In addition the indignities of poverty compound the indignities of disability. Disabled people have a sense that they are always on the receiving end, always having to ask and be grateful for the bare essentials of life. There are the indignities of being examined by doctors and others to see that their disabilities really are what they say. There is a feeling too, increased of late as a result of government policy, that the criteria for all benefits are kept as tight as possible.

This impression was given credence in April 1994 when the House of Lords ruled on the case of Eric Mallinson from Manchester. Mr Mallinson is blind and was claiming the middle-rate care component of the Disability Living Allowance, worth £30.55 a week, so that he could have a sighted person to accompany him when walking in unfamiliar areas. For years the Department of Social Security had taken a tough line on this issue, arguing that a blind person should not be paid extra by the state for having a carer to walk him or her down to the shops or to read letters as these activities were not 'normal bodily functions'. Organizations representing blind people had argued that seeing is a bodily function and it is being able to see that is the basis for requiring help. Finding in Mr Mallinson's favour, the Law Lords explicitly accepted the argument, both for that specific case and also that from now on assistance with a whole range of activities should be included when the needs of visually impaired people are being assessed for disability allowance.

Mr Mallinson said that he would have been a 'cabbage' if he had not had help in getting out and about.

The then Minister for Disabled People, William Hague, when asked about the interpretation of rules, said quite firmly that rules where they existed should be enforced or else changed by Parliament. It remains to be seen if he will introduce legislation to overturn the Law Lords' decision. If he does, say disabled people, the impression of meanness given out by the Conservative Government will be confirmed.

There are many places where individuals can go to seek advice. The Citizen's Advice Bureaux will ensure that all relevant claims are made. Charities and self-help organizations exist to make sure no benefit has been lost and, in some cases, top-up payments come from the voluntary sector. Indeed it is part of the present government's policy to involve the voluntary agencies as much as possible, especially in the area of providing care at home.

But to whom can someone turn to talk through the psychological barriers to seeking the maximum help? Many old people are fiercely proud and would not dream of seeking 'charity'. It is an ingrained notion in our society, particularly amongst the older members, that one has a duty to be independent and provide for oneself, and there is a major loss of dignity in seeking charitable help.

Christ and poverty

It is difficult to find any specific Christian advice in this area. While the notion of society having responsibility for the least well-off has evolved from the Western Christian heritage, there is very little to be found in the Bible about what it is like to be poor. It could be argued that the Gospels are written by more privileged people (a tax collector and a physician among them). They are certainly aimed at the well-off, those who need to be warned about storing up riches and to be reminded of their charitable obligations. The gospel emphasis is on the individual's response to the poverty of others, culminating in the passage in which the Christian is required to see Christ in the very poorest and least in society.

However, liberation theologians in the Third World have produced a new slant on the Gospel message and talk about identifying with the poor. They talk of the iniquities of powerful political and economic systems and identify with the struggle of poor people against them. In the famous words of Archbishop Helder Camera: 'When I feed the poor they call me a saint, when I ask why they are poor they call me a Communist.'

In the Old Testament the Jewish law anticipates how poverty can be rooted in the system, and some radical proposals exist to overcome the difficulties posed when polarizations of wealth occur. The origin of the term 'jubilee' is to be found in the Book of Leviticus. It has nothing to do with celebrating a monarch's length of reign, but with the redistribution of wealth every half century so that those who have become rich at the expense of poor people are required to right these inequalities.

Furthermore, the apostle Paul, one of the leading lights of the first Christians, regularly took up collections from wealthy church communities to support the poorer Christians in Jerusalem, and commanded other churches to follow suit; from each according to their resources, to each according to their needs.

So while the Gospels talk of individual responsibilities and responses to poverty, the Judaeo-Christian tradition requires a broader look to be taken at the systems which create inequality. There are still those of course who emphasize individual rather than corporate responsibilities, and there is in no way a clear-cut interpretation of the evidence. However, if it is acknowledged that there can be collective as well as individual wrongdoing then arguably similar forces are at work creating inequalities of opportunity against disabled people as there are creating inequalities of wealth between people.

At the root of these inequalities of wealth are inequalities of power: the powerful accumulate money and possessions, the powerless experience poverty. And with the loss of power goes the loss of self-esteem and dignity, and of the ability to choose the life one wants to live and the talents one can develop. When the liberation theologians of the Third World talk of identifying with poor, downtrodden and powerless people, they are not only talking about increasing the standards of living of the less well-off; that sole emphasis would be difficult to justify within the context of a gospel which continually under-plays the importance of money and material possessions. Identifying with poor people also involves sharing their lives, in order to raise awareness of the causes of poverty and to provide the necessary self-esteem to people who, if they can satisfy the basic needs of life and achieve self-determination, can still develop a lifestyle and culture of which they can be proud.

The European Disabled People's Parliament

In Europe, many disabled people believe that it is through pursuing political power that the inequities of the benefit systems and the ingrained structural poverty of disability will be tackled. Again, the emphasis is not simply on increasing money and employment opportunities, important as those things are, but on sharing political power and control over life. In the shorthand of the activists this means demanding civil rights.

At the end of 1993, in a powerful gesture, 350 disabled people met in Brussels on the European Day for Disabled Persons to take over the European Parliament. For a whole day disabled people set the agenda, sat in the seats normally reserved for MEPs and had all the parliamentary facilities at their disposal.

At midnight on the evening before, in a small park in the centre of Brussels, fifty of the temporary MEPs plus friends met to mark the start of Europe's special day. Despite the cold and rain, with the music of the civil rights anthem 'We Shall Overcome' as a background, Rachel Hurst of Disabled Peoples International set the tone for the day ahead.

I would like a few seconds silence, so that we can remember all those disabled people who are not with us, that we can remember all those disabled people who are in institutions against their wishes. That we can remember all those disabled people who have died without getting their human rights. Please let us have a few minutes' silence to remember them.

As the small crowd dispersed some of the delegates explained to me why they had made the journey to Brussels for the occasion.

I've come from originally in Galway in the west of Ireland. I am now living in Dublin. Why have I come here? As a person with a disability I see this sort of gathering gives a motivation to keep going in the struggle for one's human and civil rights. Things in Ireland are progressing slowly but surely. Recently the Irish government have announced a commission on the status of people with disabilities and 60 per cent of that membership is people with disabilities, it's just been announced this week, so it's very timely given the European day of disability.

I come from Naples, Italy, I come here because I think the discrimination in Europe is very big for disabled people. In Italy too now we have a very strong war against the government because it wants to tax the little money we have as disabled people for living. We want to work, we want to go to school and to go to Mass we want to be free. Independent living in Italy has a long way.

The European Disabled People's Parliament gathered at ten in the morning. Delegates met in the new semicircular debating chamber at the European Parliament, some, just for the day, taking the seats of their own MEPs. The MEPs themselves were not in evidence except for a few like Ken Coates, who chairs the European sub-committee on human rights. He gave his own welcome to the delegates, drawing their attention to the parliament building itself.

In all its colossal scope it represents a very strong commitment not only to European union but to a central problem for our democracies which is the overcoming of what is called the democratic deficit. This is a big affirmation that the democratic deficit in broad political affairs has got a short life ahead of it but you have made a new contribution to the argument because the Disabled People's Parliament is an affirmation that the other democratic deficit cannot be allowed to continue. The other democratic deficit is the maintenance of a wall of exclusion which leaves outside the discussion all kinds of social forces, all kinds of people who do not have access in the normal way to a public space, whose voices are not heard.

Simply put, unpacking the jargon of Eurospeak, the 'democratic deficit' is that gap in power and influence that exists between those who shape policy at the top and those who can do nothing but be buffeted around by the bureaucracy, unable to control their destinies.

The Disabled People's Parliament had three purposes: to provide a platform for members to talk briefly about their own countries and insights, to pass a resolution calling on the countries of Europe to support equal opportunities for disabled people and to be a forum for the signing of an affirmation of support by visitors, representatives of the nations and institutions of Europe and the European Commissioner for Social Affairs Paddy Flynn.

I sign the affirmation of commitment to the rights of disabled people. Human rights is the central issue of the debate and what these rights mean in reality for the 34 million disabled Europeans you have been nominated to represent here today. And as Commissioner responsible for Social Affairs I believe that a fundamental commitment to equal opportunities, opportunities to choose a lifestyle most suited to one's own needs, preferences, abilities and goals is essential to the achievement of full human rights for disabled people, indeed for all members of society.

The European Parliament is not like the Westminster version, it is not confrontational and those who were MEPs for the day spoke in prepared statements. It was only afterwards that they unpacked the jargon and added the colour to their arguments. Teresia Deginer is a political activist in the Disability Movement from Germany.

I think it is a very historical event. It's the first time that the European Parliament is governed or ruled by disabled people themselves. People who are the best experts on disability policy. We know what we're talking about and I hope the message I gave in the debate is that we are here to change the mind of many people and to change European policy on disability, to make a shift in paradigm from the medical rehabilitation model to the independent living model. The medical rehabilitation model I experienced was that I spent several years in an

*institution just because people wanted me to wear prosthetics,
artificial arms. I have been born without arms and ever since
used my feet and I feel very comfortable with using my feet, but
I was never allowed to do it. There are no disabled rehabilitation
experts. You are told as a disabled child that you are different
and we, the able-bodied experts, will make you almost non-
disabled if you go along with our therapy. But this meant in my
case destroying my own identity. They put shoes on I could not
open, they did not feed me when I was hungry, they beat me
up, they put me in a dark room. I mean that was over twenty
years ago. It's a long time ago but I'm sure it happens today.
Maybe they have other methods now, more psychological, more
clean methods, but they really torture people to adapt to the
non-disabled society. The independent living model however says
that we are different and as such we have the right to equality,
we have a right to be different, to look different, act different,
because that's the way we are.*

*I'm pretty sure that the way I was treated is still happening. I
counsel parents with babies without arms. Most of the parents
want their children to have prosthetics because they think it's
much better for them and the child because then the child will
look more normal. I always tell them, wait until the child can
decide by itself, let's say when it's ten or twelve years old. Until
then let's please please let him or her use her feet. The parents,
when they see me, believe me. They try to follow this advice but
the rehabilitation experts, especially doctors, put a lot of
pressure on them. They say that I am giving totally wrong
information and advice and the only reason why I do not accept
prosthetics is because we, the doctors, started too late with me.
I was three months when I got my first prosthetics but they now
start with two weeks, six weeks so that the baby grows up with
a feeling that prosthetics is part of their body.*

When asked if it was not a natural response of a mother immediately
after the birth of a child to say, 'Is the child okay; does the child have
arms, legs?' Teresia replied that the mother has to realize that she is
non-disabled.

If I become a mother I would love to have a child without arms,
but that's because I want to reproduce myself. All non-disabled
mothers want to reproduce themselves. If the child is disabled
they shouldn't put pressure on the child. The important point
that they have to realize is the view of the non-disabled looking
upon us, it's not our view of ourselves.

If I had a child I would ask, 'Is the child okay, does she not
have arms?' I would be very happy to have a child without arms.

More challenging and punchy testimony came from a delegate
from Cork in Ireland. Elaine O'Neil raised the question of the role
of charities. In Ireland she said the charitable movement was very
influential.

I think it's got something to do with the church and guilt,
that if people don't give to charity they're doing wrong.
Ireland is very charitable and we have proved that loads and
loads of times, but the only thing is that that tends to keep
disabled people boxed up where they are and it takes
responsibility away from the government so that they don't
have to legislate.

I have not been involved in fundraising for at least ten years
but I was involved in it from my early teens until I was about
twenty. I just began to feel terrible about it. I had always felt
terrible about it but I'd had enough. I couldn't really identify
why until I did a course in disability equality training, and now I
can validate my feelings. There is no way I would get involved in
any kind of negative fundraising.

In her speech to the one-day parliament Elaine O'Neil homed in on
the attitudes of able-bodied people to people like herself.

There's one school of thought that people are very sorry for us.
On the other hand there's religion and we are told by religious
people that either we're very lucky and chosen and this is our
cross in life and we're very close to God because we have a
disability or in contrast we are told that someone along our

family line has sinned a lot and we pay the price for having our disability. And there is also ridicule of us, I think people in Ireland don't like strong disabled people, they don't like empowered disabled people, so that is most people. It contradicts the image that they have already in their mind. And to be coping is to be stroppy and seen as far too independent. It's not seen as being just the same as everybody else. So it's not popular to have an opinion, to be strong, to be visible about your disability and proud of it.

Richard Wood is from the British Council of Organizations of Disabled People and he is not one to mince his words. Indeed he quoted later some particularly offensive language which had once been aimed at him.

People just feel they can say anything to you and this happens to disabled people all the time. We go for a job and get the comment, 'We don't employ fucking spastics here.' That was said at an interview to me. It's one of a series of examples I could quote of the sort of oppression, of blatant discrimination we experience. And while some people do that, there are others who are far more subtle but just as oppressive. There are people who stand and watch you while you get out of your car. People stop you in the street and they want to recount all sorts of weird and wonderful experiences they had with their great-aunt Nelly forty years ago when they were taken on holiday in a wheelchair to Skegness. They feel that they've got to recount this to you. You've got to give up the time and you mustn't get angry. And I can give you another example, it was quite a small thing but it really annoyed me. I was putting my coat on in the street and this guy rushed up and was pulling my coat on me and I was trying to get him off and this ended up in a huge argument. He felt that I should have been grateful that he was coming over to help me with my coat. I mean do you stop everybody in the street and offer to help them with their coat? You hear this all the time from disabled people.

In his statement to the parliament Richard Wood reserved his best shots for a single offensive word, 'special'.

It's a 'special' word, isn't it? I mean what 'special' usually means for us is that somebody else has got the power and somebody else makes the decisions about our lives. Basically what they're saying is we don't have a right to mainstream education, mainstream transport, housing programmes, jobs. Everywhere we look, everywhere we turn, all around us is this word 'special'. All around us are people who are employed to look after our 'special' needs, it is in itself a form of oppression and it's used to keep us in our place.

I'm a great cynic. I don't believe this struggle for our rights is about us. It's about the politicians. These people are ultimately going to have to pass legislation and there is the danger that they will pass the legislation that they want not the legislation that we want. Anyone who's had any dealings with Brussels or with Europe on any programme soon finds that they're actually on a different agenda.

One representative from Italy, Teresa Selisara, concentrated her fire on image. She told of the Italian telethon which raises hundreds of millions of lire for muscular dystrophy research and its current advertising campaign.

They are using a picture of an empty electric wheelchair and they say let's abolish this electric wheelchair. Then they say, what is it more dramatic to die in an electric chair or to live in it? And of course it's a joke of words involving the electric chair in which people are executed in America. We think that such a slogan is really terrible. It's like a psychological terrorism. It doesn't help us to give good positive images of disabled people. It doesn't say that an electric wheelchair can be an instrument of freedom.

There has been a long-standing debate on the role of people with learning disabilities within the wider disability rights movement.

Can or should people with learning disabilities be given independence and responsibilities (see also Chapter 6)? It was quite noticeable that at the parliament people with learning disabilities were badly under-represented, but Rita Lawla from Ireland was a powerful self-advocate.

People with learning difficulties or disabilities should be shown as achievers. Their talents, capabilities and work should be seen. We should not be labelled as mentally handicapped. We do not want to be hassled. We want to be able to choose like other people where and how we live. The European Parliament could do a lot for the learning difficulty people. You must listen to us because we are adults. We can speak up for ourselves and we know what we need.

While the parliament continued on through the day with over seventy of those present being given just three minutes to say their piece, some of the most revealing stories emerged in conversation outside the chamber. Sharon Mace described her experience of disability.

When I realized I just wasn't going to be able to sit up, it was affecting my education, I went to my local hospital and asked if I could have a wheelchair that I could lie down in and I was told that it didn't exist. There was nothing that they could provide me with. So I enquired how I was going to get to school, how I could continue with my 'O' level studies and they said, well, you won't be able to. People who can't sit up, stay in bed and that was at the age of thirteen. I'd just been told that because I couldn't sit up I couldn't go to school and get an education. So I went home very angry, very upset and designed a wheelchair that I could lie down in. I went straight back to the hospital workshop and the engineers designed it in their lunch hour, but they had to do it unofficially. It placed an enormous pressure on me as a young teenager having to take the services in my own hands and control my life by overriding professional adults which I shouldn't have had to do.

And she went on to explain about another very personal intrusion by professional adults into her life.

This happened but it is almost too unbelievable to be true. A doctor suggested to me that around the age of fourteen I should have a hysterectomy, because dealing with an average menstrual cycle would make life too difficult for my assistants. At the time I didn't really understand what it would entail. I just said no because I didn't like the idea of an operation. But now as a twenty-four-year-old disabled woman I'm horrified that anybody, let alone a professional who signed an oath that my health interests would be upheld, can suggest such a violation of my body. Disabled women don't have children—that was the medical feeling behind the offer.

The few politicians present, and only those with a special interest in disability attended, did not overly impress the disabled delegates. Many of the things that they said proved the point that they were addressing a different agenda. They talked in Eurojargon about the sums of money being made available for this project or that and frequently used terminology such as 'handicapped' which the delegates themselves carefully avoided. Some of the politicians relied on self-congratulation as if to say, 'How good we are to be present talking to you and look what we have managed to re-transfer by way of resources from our social budgets to help people like you.'

Rachel Hurst chaired the parliament and introduced the MEPs and Commissioner, and addressed the subject of the gulf in political perception between the able-bodied politicians and the disabled activists.

I think that not everybody's concept of us is as members of a civil rights movement. I think they see us as people who are in need. What we are trying to say is that that's not the issue. Yes we're in need, but we're in need of our civil rights, civil and human rights. We're not in need for a whole lot of services which we didn't want in the first place.

I think it takes a long time, it actually takes a disabled person quite a long time to articulate where the oppression's coming from. But there are many able-bodied people who are allies and they are essential. We can't do without our allies. We need them, but what we also need to do is to continue to educate them totally.

I remember the moment in my own life when it gelled for me as a political issue. It was as soon as I went out in a wheelchair. I had been going through various stages of stumbling around, being thought drunk, using a stick and so on. But once I used a wheelchair I was completely denied access to other human beings. It was incredible. Friends I'd known for years just walked on the other side of the road. That made me see instantly the oppression. Interestingly it opened my eyes too to my oppression as a woman, so now I fight on both fronts.

And she added with a chuckle, 'I'm an awful person to live with.'

The European Disabled People's Parliament came to an end after just one day in which members had sat briefly in the seats of power.

Blessed are the activists?

To take part in political activity at any level is not for the retiring type. It requires the ability to stand up, be heard and to push oneself forward. In the struggle for what is perceived as justice and a fair distribution of power, those involved in the political hurly-burly have to believe they can justify the self-promotion required. Fortunately politics is not just left to the egotists and self-publicists. There are others who have important contributions to make. But before they can get too involved they must face in their own minds the contradiction presented by Jesus' Sermon on the Mount. For that teaching states clearly that it is the *meek* who are blessed, or truly happy. Can a person required to practise the skills of politics really be approved in the Christian framework?

Arguably yes, for those who 'hunger and thirst for righteousness' are also promised true happiness. There certainly seems no contradiction in pursuing just cases associated with disability politics and the teaching of the Gospels as seen in this light.

In practical terms, the call for rights involves pressure on governments and social agencies to allow disabled people control and responsibility over their own lives. It arises from those assorted feelings of impatience, frustration and indignity which can arise from being someone constantly on the receiving end of care.

One very practical solution is for disabled people to have spending power. Before it was abruptly brought to an end, the Independent Living Fund enabled many severely disabled people to receive money for their care and to have the choice as to how that money was spent.

For various reasons, some of them to do with finance, the fund stopped taking new applicants and was restructured to allow local authorities a much greater say in how the care-users lives' were organized.

Yet a study undertaken by the University of Greenwich clearly showed that where disabled people are given responsibility to make care choices using their own finances it is more cost-effective. Perhaps there was a hidden agenda at play when the Independent Living Fund was abolished; that the professionals could not handle the idea that they were no longer in charge.

For, to quote the words of the Greenwich report, where users have control over how their support needs are met it provides

a good model for the empowerment of disabled people by demonstrating that, given genuine choice and adequate resources, disabled people are able to exercise control over their own lives and reduce for themselves their enforced dependency on inadequate services.

There is no doubt that when community services have to be used disabled people find their life choices severely restricted. They can get up in the morning or go to bed at night only when the local carers say they can. They have to fit in to a tight timetable organized by someone else.

To quote one of the community service users interviewed in the Greenwich survey:

The home helps were very limited and you had to fit in with them at all times. The Community Care Attendant Scheme is more flexible but you have to accept the times of day that are

pre-arranged and the same for the length of visits, you are
limited a lot by the rota system used. If you do not get on with
anyone sent to you, you have to accept this, as they don't seem
to employ enough people to not send particular individuals (due
to sickness/leave etc of staff) that you do not happen to hit it
off with.

In contrast, those disabled people with the means to buy and control their own help talked enthusiastically about the greater flexibility it gave them.

One woman, for instance, said she had been saved from going into an institution. Another said,

I am a mother again. My son is again a child—he should never
have had to empty a commode for his mother—or cook and
clean for us both... I do not have to use my friends any more. I
can go to the shops myself—I can go out when I want to—I can
sleep upstairs in my own room and get up to go to the toilet
instead of sleeping next to a commode. Quality of life—great.
I'm alive again—free.

To rework the European jargon, the power deficit has been reduced. Power, however, involves responsibility. For people to take responsibility and to be given responsibility is not incompatible with a wider understanding of a right and just society. But for more disabled people to be empowered, to be released from the trap of the poverty of low self-esteem and reliance, requires certain major shifts in attitude. It requires society to rethink its image of disabled people as the needy and those requiring charity. But for that change to come about we need to realize why mainstream society needs to have this image. For when disabled people are disempowered, the rest feel powerful. And power tends to corrupt.

6

MIND AND SPIRIT

Physically disabled people are highly sensitive—and rightly so—to imputations that their disabilities make them incapable of living life to the full. But what about those with learning difficulties? Should they have rights too?

Shortly after the highly successful Paralympic Games were held in Barcelona in 1992, athletes from around the world converged on Madrid for another sporting extravaganza. This time, however, the sportsmen and -women were not physically disabled but had been labelled or diagnosed as having learning difficulties.

It is hard to know what term to use these days for people with Down's Syndrome and other conditions which would once have been termed mental handicap, for 'learning difficulties' is a term which was once acceptable, but now throws up a number of other problems. One has difficulties in learning if one is deaf or has dyslexia, but that does not qualify for inclusion within the term 'mental handicap'. 'Learning disabilities' is a current favourite, but while whatever expression is used will never be perfect, it is bound to be preferable to such derogatory classifications as 'idiot' or 'moron' which were used quite widely a century ago.

As physically disabled athletes look forward to Atlanta in 1996 and the next Paralympic Games, an acrimonious debate has been brewing. Back in 1992 the sports governing bodies decided that in future all disabled athletes, whether physically disabled or with learning disabilities, should take part in the same event. There would still be classifications separating them out when it came to individual races or contests, but in general it was felt the statement should be made that there should be no division within the world of disability.

Many of the Paralympic athletes objected and were vociferous in their criticisms of the idea, some using language which they later had cause to retract. Sponsors too baulked at the proposal. Some thought the image of mentally handicapped athletes on the screen would devalue the more attractive image projected by the elite of the wheelchair racing corps, an image which they had spent so long cultivating.

At the time of writing the issue is unresolved, but it does illustrate a clear division in approach. As strongly as many physically disabled people will argue for empowerment, choice and equal rights, they do not include those with learning disabilities. These people, it is assumed, are not capable of taking decisions for themselves. They are seen to be too irresponsible, simple or unsophisticated, not only to be capable of taking control of their lives, but also of expressing preferences and ambitions.

The right response

Where can one turn for a wider view on this issue? There would appear to be no advice given in the Christian scriptures. Indeed in the New Testament, while people with mental illness, physical disability and disease are well represented, nowhere is a person with learning disabilities mentioned. Perhaps in those days they were kept out of sight, although, judging from other pre-industrial societies this would have been unusual—in many cases, families absorbed such people quite naturally and the community followed suit, even if on some occasions the individual with learning disabilities became seen as the village idiot or mascot. And the record of subsequent centuries does not show any improvement on this attitude.

As David Potter observed in his book *Mental Handicap*,

The picture of the past is rather discouraging. It has to be said that, by and large, Christians have shown serious disregard for people with mental handicaps.

For guidance and inspiration one needs to look to such twentieth-century figures as Jean Vanier, the founder of the L'Arche communities where disabled and able-bodied people live together on equal terms. In the publisher's resumé of his book *Be Not Afraid* his approach is described in these terms:

> *The simplicity of the central Christian message is stark in its clarity: 'love your neighbour as yourself'. But carrying out this demand is a less simple matter. Among the difficulties encountered is that of fear—fear to let go of personal habits and ingrained attitudes; fear of the unknown outside our limited experiences; fear of the extent of self-commitment which is required.*
>
> *Jean Vanier writes with sympathy and understanding of this stranglehold of fear upon the good intentions of so many Christians, dealing with it tolerantly, perceptively and with constant reference to the New Testament. And besides showing how fear in all its forms can undermine ordinary human relationships, he gives many heartening instances of genuine attempts being made at living in Christian community.*

This view is amplified and given flesh by Jean Vanier's sister, Dr Terese Vanier, writing about Nick Ellerker, a man with Down's Syndrome who spent fourteen years as a member of the L'Arche community. Nick was said to have had a remarkable personality and life. He was no angel but was endowed with gifts of the heart. It was said of him that he had a passion for reconciliation and unity, and that his life had an extraordinary effect on all who encountered him through his simplicity, profound spirituality and rumbustious humanity.

Certainly the L'Arche community has been inspirational in producing a change in perspective. Its founder had been horrified by visiting an institution in France where eighty men with learning disabilities lived in what he described as a 'chaotic atmosphere of violence and uproar'. The conviction grew in him that 'Jesus wanted something to be done'.

Others have followed Vanier's example and today there are many places, inspired by the Christian ethic, where people with learning difficulties can lead fulfilled lives, including the opportunity to explore faith. Recently I had the chance to attend a service at Yately parish church in Hampshire being led by members of the Causeway group. This group included a number of members with learning disabilities who led prayers and singing and performed a short play to illustrate the Gospel reading. While many people with learning disabilities do attend church on a regular basis, it is rare for them to be leading the worship. The congregation at Yately proved most welcoming and willing, not only to participate in the spirit of the service but to learn from the new insights on offer. As Sally Martin of the Causeway group said at the time, reflecting on her career in the theatre:

On the stage we all wore masks. We kept our true selves hidden behind a character or an act.

With Causeway there are no masks. A person with learning difficulties has no need for the sophisticated social veneer behind which most 'normal' people spend their lives and the real loving human being shines through.

However, it is argued forcibly, and in some cases irrefutably, that, regardless of endearing personal qualities, many people with learning difficulties do not have the capacity to function in the normal material world. Sometimes even such day to day tasks as dressing and washing appear to be beyond them and even with people who can take domestic responsibility, dealing with money and property can present seemingly insurmountable hurdles. Many carers and parents are fearful of what might happen if responsibilities beyond the individual's capability were handed over. What disasters might befall? Might an individual find the wrong friends, get seriously in debt, or even accidentally burn the house down?

Yet it does not mean that because someone may find it difficult to take certain responsibilities that they should be prevented from expressing preferences and making choices. To enable them to do this, people with learning disabilities may need the assistance of an advocate, someone who can spend time to explain the choices available and understand the individual's preferences. The advocate then speaks for them. Alternatively, self-advocacy skills can be taught to many. It is a mistake to assume that adults with learning difficulties do not have opinions, simply because they find it difficult to formulate and express them.

Learning to speak up

In the spring of 1994 I visited a group of adults with learning difficulties being taught how to speak up for themselves and put their point of view. The group was called 'Ask Us', and it met fortnightly in North London. A dozen or so people, over a cup of coffee, chat, tell each other news and talk about their problems and worries, with the guidance of a facilitator.

I spoke to Linda and David, who told me about the group and the news they had to share that week. They talked about how they had been shopping, in particular how they had been to get a farewell card for their facilitator Alan Steer, who was about to leave for a new job.

Alan told me how the group was funded by social services and other agencies and what happens to people who join up.

In the long run I think what happens is that people become more confident in themselves and they become more aware of what their opinions are. A lot of people will join the group and not even be aware of what opinions they have or equally will come along and give the answer which they think that you want to hear.

Some people become very angry and upset when they get involved in self-advocacy and this is something that it is important we explain to people, especially carers, mums and dads. Some people will get quite upset and act inappropriately when they start with self-advocacy because, maybe for the first time in their adult lives, they're really speaking up for themselves, but don't know yet quite how to go about that. And people go through that period of anger and upset and inappropriate behaviour and then gradually come out the other side still with strong feelings, but putting those strong feelings in more appropriate ways.

In due course 'Ask Us' group members will graduate to being involved as co-ordinators and support workers, helping to organize transport and making sure members are able to get to meetings.

It would be a mistake to assume that adults with learning difficulties simply need to practise the basics, to learn how to choose what to buy or what to wear. Often serious problems arise for people without the confidence to form an opinion or state it firmly. One group member told me what happened to him back in 1985 when he was working at a local hospital.

One of the workers that worked there approached me and he quite plainly said would you be interested in what is known as sexual intercourse and in those days I didn't know whether to say no or yes. So I was a bit bewildered.

So I said quite plainly alright carry on then. He took me somewhere and it went on and on and on and on until 1988 or 1989 when then I had to decide whether to let the thing continue or go and report it to someone.

So eventually I decided, right that's it I'm going to report it. So I had to go and see the manager who worked at the hospital and he said to me you've done the right thing to come along and speak to me, because if I'd carried on and on and on right up to this year, it would have got so worse, I would probably have had a nervous breakdown.

It was through joining 'Ask Us' that that member in particular acquired the confidence to share his distressing story publicly and he will no doubt in future react very differently if presented with a similar problem.

Bearing in mind that every disabled individual has a unique experience of life and a unique set of talents and abilities, many people with learning difficulties can live very ably in society with just a little appropriate support.

However, frequently in the past, patterns of care have not reflected this and individuals have either been over-protected and never given a chance to thrive as independent citizens, or, conversely, left entirely and inappropriately to fend for themselves. Getting the right balance is not easy, but the London KeyRing project, which I visited on behalf of 'Does He Take Sugar?', is providing a successful model.

Good neighbours

Michelle Warner knows what it is like to be homeless in London. She knows what it is like to beg for money to buy food and to have nowhere to sleep at night but a doorway. At one time she did not even have a blanket to keep her warm or the cardboard for a makeshift bed and so stayed up all night shivering in her clothes.

Michelle has learning difficulties and she was educated at a school for pupils with special needs. School-days were not an easy time for her but she learnt the hard way, when she began to fend for herself, that life was much tougher on the outside.

I used to be brought in by the coppers and put in the police cells and once had two nights at an emergency shelter but then left and found myself on the streets again.

It was with people like Michelle in mind that, four years ago, community worker Carl Poll set about creating the KeyRing network. He realized that there were many hundreds of people with moderate learning difficulties who could live independent lives in ordinary houses if only there was a reliable good neighbour to hand. He felt the old-style approach, of building hostels where people with learning difficulties lived side by side, was not always the solution. The KeyRing network scheme which he devised was much simpler, more cost-effective and, as it has turned out, popular with those it was designed to help.

Michelle now lives in a flat as a tenant in the Wandsworth KeyRing network. Not far away is her friend Millie Butler, a KeyRing tenant of long standing, and within about five minutes walking distance there are seven other tenants. They do not live on top of each other and they pursue independent lives, but they exist to help each other out in emergencies, with help, friendly advice and guidance from another neighbour, support worker Phil Pescud. He lives in a block of flats in the same area and is paid by KeyRing to devote ten hours a week to seeing that his nine near neighbours are coping. He is there to answer any questions and sort out any problems. Millie and Michelle both like the scheme.

I used to see Phil a lot when I first started. Now I see him only now and again. He used to moan at me for not doing this and that but now I've got myself sorted out with the gas meters and everything else, I don't need to see him so often.

He helps me out with reading and writing and forms and things like that. He'll pop round and I know I can go and see him if I need anything.

Not far away Stuart Long has his own flat. Until four years ago Stuart, 45, lived with his mother, with whom he had lived all his life. When she died his whole world fell apart.

She used to look after me, perhaps she mollycoddled me. But when she died I was all over the place, I couldn't do things for myself.

After a difficult period of adjustment, Stuart now has his own second-floor flat, works as a floor porter at a top London hotel and, with regular calls from Phil, is coping well.

I shop at Asda, do my washing at the launderette and got new clothes at the January sales.

It costs approaching £20,000 a year to run a KeyRing network with nine tenants. Initially the money was found by the Joseph Rowntree Foundation and now KeyRing, as a registered charity, is seeking contracts with local councils through Carl Poll.

Compared with keeping a person with learning difficulties in residential accommodation, the KeyRing is extremely cost-effective. Not only can tenants turn to Phil or the support worker but they also have each other. If one of them for instance locks him or herself out at night, there's always a sofa to sleep on nearby until the problem can be sorted out in the morning.

In the past many people with learning difficulties have been given flats but have then, in effect, been abandoned to their own loneliness, fears and problems. By belonging to a network tenants still retain and value their independence, but also get the support they need. Most of them have been referred to KeyRing by agencies and local authorities but KeyRing encourages people to refer themselves if they feel they can benefit from the scheme.

When we contract our services to local councils it might not be possible for individuals to refer themselves in the same way. This would be a bad move.

There are five schemes up and running in London at the moment and Carl hopes the idea will spread to other parts of the country. It is a practical model for care in the community which has proved to be extremely effective. The scheme has been monitored closely and has had an overwhelming vote of confidence from the tenants.

Unique abilities

Once settled and independent many people with learning difficulties find, for the first time, that they have talents and gifts which are valued. These may be in the form of friendship and loyalty or, as I discovered on a visit to Glasgow in 1993, in artistic and creative potential.

I went to see the Glasgow showing of a travelling art exhibition featuring pictures by artists with learning disabilities. It was an international show and the British contribution to the exhibition had come largely from the Glasgow-based arts organization Project Ability. I met Margaret Murphy who had recently visited Belgium to paint posters for the Project 12 exhibition, who told me what she liked to paint.

I like painting different things. I did one of rock around the clock and that was with Elvis, Buddy Holly, the Righteous Brothers. The big guitar and the LPs and the wee singles and also the big fifties juke box and it lets them see what era it was in.

Cameron Morgan had painted the Project 12 poster at Kelvingrove, a colourful work which matched his enthusiasm for art.

I do ceramics and I did a mosaic for Glasgow Royal Infirmary and it's a big huge thing.

Did he know what the final picture would look like before starting on a major commission, or did the image come spontaneously?

I just more or less take it as it comes. I'd done one or two wee sketches to see if I liked it.

Elizabeth Gibson is the project's director who showed me round the workshop and told me more about the thinking behind Project Ability.

Project Ability works with people who are in some way marginalized through reasons of disability, through reasons of ill health, through reasons of social circumstances, young people and elderly people, really a very wide base within the community. They are people who perhaps wouldn't think of trying to test their creative skills normally.
In many cases we often discover that we're working with people who are very able and very confident, have lots of experience in using arts and our role then is a supportive one.

Gordon Cumming had taken full advantage of the opportunities. He is a writer, is involved in contemporary drama, as well as being a painter.

It's something to do that I had never done before. I'd never got a chance to do before. I've also done a bit of drawing and painting and I actually managed to get one of my paintings sold in London, so I was quite happy with that. First time I've ever done that actually get a painting sold.

Elizabeth Gibson is proud of the project's achievements.

Every person who we've ever met has been able to bring something unique to the project and that can be a very small achievement or it can be quite an outstanding artistic achievement, but for each person it's something which is quite individual to that person. People who perhaps worked with us initially now will independently come to our centre. These are often people who a year ago, two years ago couldn't get the bus into town by themselves, they will have achieved that and they will have developed these skills because they have chosen to come to our centre to continue to do their art work.

No sex please, you're disabled

The assumption that disabled people are, or should be asexual is most noticeable in relation to people with learning disabilities. People with Down's Syndrome, in particular, appear to bring out in their parents and teachers a special prurient protectiveness. When this was recently challenged in a a television drama showing the courtship of two people with Down's Syndrome, there was a lively debate. What if things got out of hand?... and they had sex?

In their study *Parenting under Pressure*, Tim and Wendy Booth explored the way in which society at large treats parents with learning difficulties. The results of their research make disturbing reading. Some parents lived in constant fear of abuse from neighbours, inappropriate interference from authorities and even threat of their children being taken from them. Many of these parents needed some support but most of the problems they faced related to the social conditions and the financial poverty of their lives rather than specifically to their learning difficulties. Indeed, it could be pointed out that many highly intelligent and capable adults in good financial circumstances make very cold and inadequate parents, yet seldom are they subjected to the same forms of intrusion.

Tim and Wendy relate the story of Molly Austin, struggling with life in a cold caravan with her partner Kevin and two children, one aged four and the other three. Molly has learning difficulties and is unable to read.

Molly's apparent shortcomings as a mother have to be seen in the context of her own upbringing and the pressures currently bearing down on her. She grew up in institutions and never had the opportunity to acquire many domestic skills... had no experience of an ordinary family life nor any role models on which to base her own parenting behaviour.

Molly is the victim of gendered assumptions by Kevin and by service workers that unjustly show her up in a bad light... Molly has received little parenting support from the health and welfare services. Service delivery tends to be crisis orientated: Molly has been left to cope as best she can until things go wrong. Her past experience has taught her to be wary of social workers who, in any case, tend to move on so frequently as to prevent the formation of trusting relationships. The community nurses have provided valuable practical and emotional support but often too little and too late. For example, efforts were made to help Molly with her reading but the support was not sustained until she had the confidence to go alone. There is a tendency for these shortcomings in the services to be personalized and the blame pinned on Molly. It is not so much that she has failed as that she has not been given a chance to succeed.

Tim and Wendy conclude:

A 'deficiency orientation' underpins the presumption of incompetence that fosters an expectation of parenting failure among practitioners. It also encourages the mistake of seeing parents' problems entirely in terms of their own limitations, so blaming the victims for difficulties that owe more to the pressures in their lives and the constraints of their situation. In terms of professional practice and service delivery, this approach exhibits a number of characteristic features. Assessment and review tend to lay stress on finding out what people cannot do, and to define them in terms of their deficiencies and failings. Planning is primarily resource-led, with people being fitted into existing services rather than services being designed to fit their needs. Case management *relies on professional judgment and decision-making and allows little scope for user choice and participation.*

Molly Austin's story shows how such attitudes and practices may originate, how they are sustained, and how they may be overcome in order to pave the way for a more positive approach. Practitioners or researchers who adopt a 'deficiency perspective' are led ineluctably into attributing Molly's plight and her problems to her own limitations and lack of competence. In contrast, by acknowledging her skills and the impact of environmental and social pressures on her ability to cope, a 'capacity perspective' reveals new options for practical help and support.

Research has shown that the attitude of people providing support for parents with learning difficulties is one of the key factors determining its success. A 'deficiency orientation' relegates people to a dependent status as passive recipients of services. A 'capacity perspective' would recognize Molly's resourcefulness and seek ways for her to deal with her rent arrears. Her problems are not the result of lack of competence but stem primarily from lack of money. Dealing with Molly's debts would offer her choices and enable her to re-assert control over her life. It would also allow the family to remain together. Families can be set up to fail or helped to overcome.

Whether a family or individual is set up to fail or helped to overcome largely depends on the outside world's perception. People with learning difficulties hear all too often, 'You can forget all those ideas,' from medical and support professionals. It is enlightening when the reaction is reversed, 'You may have problems but there's no reason why we can't help you lead as full a life as you want.'

7

THE DISABILITY DEBATE

Disability is seen from many points of view. People who are disabled, like any other people, will not all agree about their situation and the proper response to it, let alone have the same ideas about God and disability.

The view of disability and disability pride outlined in earlier chapters is the fashionable one among activists. However, equating disability rights with civil rights is not the way the majority of people view the subject, although in time the new ways of thinking may percolate through to public awareness.

It is always a worthwhile exercise, when watching how new ideas turn into received wisdom, to explore the views of people who have thought deeply around the subject to a point where they feel, from a position of experience and knowledge, they can challenge the fashionable notions.

Unfashionable ideas

One such person is Sam Gallop, one of the founders of the organization Opportunities for People with Disabilities, which exists to bring employers and disabled people together so that more people with disabilities can enter the world of work.

I first met Sam back in 1978 when I was involved in making a television programme about the Guinea Pig Club. Later I co-authored a book with Peter Williams, which included a section telling Sam's story. Like his fellow Guinea Pigs he had been badly injured in a flying accident during the Second World War, and had been treated at the famous East Grinstead Hospital under Sir Archibald McIndoe. Both his legs were amputated and he had a series of difficult operations to restructure his face. Later Sam returned to academic studies at Oxford, joined the electricity industry and rose to a senior position within the Central Electricity Generating Board. But his own career success did not result in him forgetting an early lesson he learnt firsthand: that many disabled people are likely to come face to face with discrimination for the first time when going for a job.

On the programme 'Does He Take Sugar?' he drew on his own experience.

I think my experience of discrimination, for want of a better word, although the person concerned was intending to be kind, started before I left university when I was trying to get my first job. I'd been writing to a major company for about six months, I filled in all the application forms, they'd all been returned, I had an interview and then there was silence. I got in touch with them. I 'phoned, I was told it was all proceeding etc. Nothing happened at all and I was getting a bit desperate, because I was getting near my finals and really hadn't got anywhere settled. And it was my tutor who opened my eyes when she simply said, 'Well, Sam, they simply don't want to say no to you.' And I found out afterwards that the job involved working in hot climates that I couldn't cope with, but in a way, trying to be kind, the personnel officer in the company, hadn't wanted to say no to me because he thought I would be very discouraged. Whereas what he should have done was be very crisp, very clear, very decisive and said, 'Look, this is not your job, we're sorry, you'll have to look elsewhere.' But I lost six months because of that.

Back in 1978 Sam Gallop was himself pioneering many of the ideas which have now become generally accepted. This comes through from reading his own words of seventeen years ago.

However magnificent the building, if the door's too narrow to take a wheelchair, a certain small percentage of people won't ever be able to get into it. Which is unfair.

However wonderful the view, if there's no lift big enough to accommodate the disabled, this same small percentage won't be able to scale the mountain to share the experience. Which is also unfair.

And it needs only a little thinking time, at the planning stage, to remedy the situation and prevent the disabled feeling like second-class citizens. After all, nobody asks to be disabled.

He referred to a classic case of a woman who went in a wheelchair to a hotel which was very proud of its suite containing a full toilet and bathroom facility for disabled people.

Unfortunately, she had to send for a carpenter to take the door off the bathroom because somebody had forgotten that the bathroom door took an inch off the access so that the wheelchair couldn't quite get through.

I think it would be good for most professional people, as part of their training, to experience a week—and I do mean a week; a solid seven days and nights in their bedroom as well—in a wheelchair, imagining that they had lost the use of their legs. I think we would see tremendous improvements.

Seventeen years ago Sam Gallop was also talking of the dangers of sympathy, especially the sympathy commonly shown to disabled people.

When you're in a hospital bed, a warm, tender feeling coming to you from the girl who is nursing you, and from the doctor, is essential to recovery. If you are feeling ghastly and you are given the right treatment, by being shaved and sat up in bed, you can look around and take a fresh view of life. After that, however, sympathy has got to be rather subtle.

It is very difficult for those responsible for rehabilitation to stand back from the people they are trying to help, and hold

*back their own feelings of sympathy and concern. They
mustn't wallow in sympathy. They should decide matters
almost dispassionately if that's possible. I am afraid that a
lot of the energy that goes into caring would be far better
converted into the energy of effective action. People care
but they don't see. They don't see the real need and I think
it is the patient, more than anyone else, who has to help
them to see.*

A disabled person soon learns about the new limits imposed on his
or her life. Everyone has limits, but a disability changes the boundaries.
What annoys Sam Gallop today is the way others impose limits without
the consent of the disabled person. He gave this example in the 'Does
He Take Sugar?' interview.

*I've had a phone call today from a young lady who's got visual
impairment who is designing and weaving altar cloths for
Westminster Abbey and she's done this for other cathedrals.
She has terrific genius and I did ask her, knowing this interview
was coming up, 'How d'you feel about the word disability or
being classed as disabled?' And she replied very forcefully, 'It's a
terrible word... people put limits on you, and I think that sums it
up. If you have this tag or this label of disability on you, which is
a negative word, other people, most certainly other people who
haven't got your type of disability, will put limits on you. And
much worse than that, they will almost put you in a position
where you're going to set yourself too low a target for what
you're going to achieve.'*

Is there not another school of thought, I suggested, particularly
voiced by people with disabilities who take a pride in their disability, that
they see they can be part of a disability subculture which has a whole
vigorous life of its own?

*I can live with that if it's done with a sense of humour. I don't
have any time at all for a subculture of people who make a
heavy issue about disability and politics and so forth, I feel they*

are achieving the opposite of what they set out to do and that you'll end up with segregation not integration.

Can one indeed actually talk about disability in these general terms at all?

No I don't think so, it makes me very uneasy. It's like vast generalizations about nations and populations and so on. I believe you have to talk about each individual person very much as an individual and talk about what they can achieve, not what they can't achieve and separate that type of discussion from the discussion about their medical needs, what some people term the medical model.

Sam Gallop is wary of any of the wide generalizations used by the disability lobby. He accepts that there are changes needed in the way able-bodied individuals react to those with a disability but puts emphasis on the disabled person acting as a catalyst for positive change.

I don't believe in large debates about disability and segregation and integration. I find them very exhausting. I don't find them at all helpful to people with disabilities in getting on with daily life. It's obvious that you've got to have a basic disability income and there's a lot more to be done in that area, but having got that settled I think one has to go out in a positive way and achieve change and that you won't achieve that through rule books and laws and so on, I think we've got plenty of legislation around the place. It's really getting down to changing individual attitudes.

Sam Gallop advocates the direct approach to counter cloying sentimentality.

A good burst of natural spontaneous healthy anger by the recipient is the best way of dealing with it and if the person goes on being cloyingly sentimental or doesn't change then just distance yourself from them, it's their loss not yours.

But it can often surely be within a family that some of the sentimentality and the restrictions which are placed upon a disabled person are found? They emanate from others in the family trying to be protective.

If that goes on then you must leave home and distance yourself from it because you are going to be socially handicapped even though with the best will in the world they are trying to protect you and trying to help you. I think we all go through this. Disability isn't special in this and it's not special in many areas. If people really want to grow up they have to leave home and if you have a disability you may have to do it sooner rather than later. Talk to people with a similar disability to your own who've got on, who've achieved things, ask them how they did it, what the barriers were and seek their help and guidance in opening doors for yourself. They're the best people to go to, people who've met the difficulties themselves.

Much of Sam Gallop's work has been in creating employment opportunities for people with disabilities. How does he go about improving attitudes within the workplace?

Once the disabled person is in employment I don't find significant difficulties in improving attitudes within the workplace. The attitudes among employees are, in my experience, excellent, down to earth and practical. In fact I think the Americans call it the 'buddy system', and from my own experience when I first started work I benefited from this. I had to be going to the limb centre quite a lot, and I could usually manage to do this say between 9 o'clock and 10.30 in the morning and I knew that my buddies were quietly covering my telephone. My work did get done but it wasn't an obvious issue and I very rarely had to go in to a 'boss' and say that I had to go to hospital the next day, would that be all right?

But I think we're talking about totally different problems if you're talking about influencing the attitude of employers where you need a continual vigorous marketing campaign. You need monitoring. You must measure achievements but at the same time I think you musn't over-measure because we are talking about human beings and without measuring there is a lot of positive discrimination in favour of disabled employees in the market-place. You just have to keep on plugging away. You're never going to do away with prejudice, and if you think you are, you're naive. What you've got to do is go out and tackle it in every possible way like any other business problem that has to be solved. Some people can be very unprejudiced in a certain area and very prejudiced in another. And I think that some people are going to be prejudiced all their lives. You're not going to change them. Those people you avoid. You don't waste time.

Rights or wrongs?

It was inevitable that after the high profile protests by the civil rights lobby in the summer of 1994 and the public embarrassments of the then minister Nicholas Scott who had to admit to having misled Parliament, that there would be a backlash in the Tory press to the notion of legal rights for disabled people. There was even a feeling of resentment that disabled people should be seeking special 'privileges'. After writing a particularly trenchant article in the *Daily Telegraph* questioning the whole notion of 'rights' Clifford Longley was invited by 'Does He Take Sugar?' in June 1994 to test his views in the company of two people at the forefront of the campaign; Rachel Hurst from the British Council of Organizations of Disabled People and Mike Oliver, Professor of Disability Studies at the University of Greenwich. Kati Whittaker chaired the discussion.

Clifford Longley began the debate.

We ought to be prepared to tolerate a system which discriminates in favour of disabled people, but in fact the essential argument about civil rights is that there should be no discrimination; there should be equality. I think the introduction of those concepts 'discrimination' and 'equality' into this is not going to help us. That's basically my objection to the way in which the language has been taken over by a rather American-style civil rights debate which I don't think works in this country.

Rachel Hurst took issue.

I would like to challenge the idea that special dispensation is what we require and what we should be satisfied with, we don't want special advantages, we actually do want to get a level playing-field, we want to get to the starting point of a race in the same way as everybody else and that's what we mean by civil rights.

But would disabled people have more rights than the able-bodied if the Civil Rights Bill went through? Mike Oliver replied.

The evidence is quite clear that the standard of living that disabled people have in Britain and indeed all over the world is far worse than the standard of living of everybody else. Government figures show that disabled people are far more likely to be unemployed, they're far more likely to be living in poverty, they're far more likely to have an inferior education and so on and so forth. Many disabled people in this country still do not have the basic rights to decide what time they'll get up in the morning, what time they'll go to bed at night and some of them do not still even have the basic human rights to decide when they will open their bladder and their bowels, now if we think that's acceptable in a modern society, if we think that we can actually resolve that problem by relying on charities and so on I'm afraid the only people who think that are those who are not likely to be in that situation. Disabled people for the last fifteen to twenty years have demonstrated the bankruptcy of those old ideas and those old ways.

We need legislation to protect disabled people from discrimination but there is a broader issue which is, do we need a Bill of Rights to protect everybody? And my answer to that, as an individual, would be an unequivocal yes.

At that point Clifford Longley interjected.

Can I correct one thing that Mike seemed to be implying, that I was against, or I was accusing disabled people of enjoying privileges that they should not enjoy. In fact I'm entirely in the opposite camp from that. I think disabled people should have privileges. All I'm saying is that discrimination in favour of disabled people is not the same thing as equality.

But disabled people do not want privileges. If you just take the area of employment, disabled people do not want to work because they're disabled. The slogan is that disabled people want access to the same unemployment rates as everyone else. Disabled people are not asking to have jobs because they're disabled, what they're saying is that they would like the labour market to operate in a way that treats them fairly and equitably so that at the end of the day if the unemployment rate amongst the population at large is 10 per cent then we'd like the unemployment rate amongst disabled people to be 10 per cent.

Clifford Longley asked,

Are we saying the same thing but using different language? We are actually aiming at the same thing, are we not?

But we're not talking about privilege. Privilege is something over and above what other people have. We're talking about coming to the same level.

Clifford Longley suggested,

Can we call it special treatment? Can we get rid of this word privilege which seems to be causing us the trouble and can we say special treatment? We all agree that there should be special treatment for disabled people.

No, we are asking for equality.

Clifford Longley persisted,

But integration into society is only achievable by singling out specific areas where special treatment should be available.

Rachel Hurst pointed out:

The whole thing around the gender regulations are that the workplace particularly should be made available to women and special things are put in place in order for that to happen, child care, special flexi-hours and all the rest of it. That's exactly the same sort of thing we're asking for, there's no difference.

Later Mike Oliver put a further point.

We're not here to have a narrow seminar about the definition of rights. The practical realities are that disabled people can't get on buses and they think they have, call it what you like, a right, a freedom, a privilege or whatever you call it, that there should be a mechanism which enables them to get on to the buses regardless of what you call it. We shouldn't subsume these real political material issues into a debate on semantics.

The whole purpose of legislation, as far as the disability movement in this country is concerned, is that we are trying to change people's behaviour. We've seen fifty years of government policy which has been targeted at changing people's attitudes and it's failed utterly and miserably as far as disabled people are concerned, just the same as it failed in terms of things like trying to change people's attitudes to wearing seat-belts. We're fed up with government spending our money on trying to change attitudes when what we consider as important are people's behaviour, and disabled people as a group now are sufficiently empowered not to be overly concerned about people's attitudes. But I do think one of the things that I would say is that in the main people are much more supportive to us and to our issues than might be supposed.

But I think also, we need to make the point that what the civil rights legislation will do is transfer much public expenditure which is currently being spent on keeping disabled people segregated and in dependence, into enabling them to come out to participate fully in society, to accept their responsibilities as citizens as well as to take their rights. It's an economically rational argument; that's the argument that swayed Congress in the States and it's the argument that we will win in Britain as well.

Clifford Longley acknowledged:

One argument I find most persuasive, if I may say so.

So how far should disabled people go with their protests? Is there a case for political disobedience? Rachel Hurst thought so.

We have all been struggling for so long to get our message across and we're desperate. There was a young girl on television the other day, a sixteen-year-old, who in tears said, 'If we don't have this legislation I have nothing to look forward to.' And that really is the situation, there are thousands of disabled people who are not getting out of their homes or doing anything. We have to stop this apartheid system.

Mike Oliver agreed with some heat:

When you have a system which calls itself democratic, where the only people who are against civil rights legislation are John Major, Michael Heseltine and a few civil servants who work in the Treasury and a few people who are employed as right-wing leader-writers for the Daily Telegraph *and* The Times *and everyone else is in favour of it, we still haven't got legislation, what are disabled people supposed to do?*

Despite the heat, the debate also produced some light, in particular, the concern that militancy pursued by disabled people could alienate the majority and undermine their whole cause. Of course the debate was conducted as a secular one. One of the dangers of disability awareness being a secular movement is that activists may not have the sensitivities required to take people gently from their old way of seeing things to a different way.

The theology of disability

In the churches, however, a re-examination of the theology of disability is very much in its early stages. Soon it will gather momentum, and dangers lie ahead. Like their secular counterparts the militant liberation theologians of disability may well alienate many in the mainstream. Their approach will have to be one of sensitivity, for the Christian debate on disability will touch many raw nerves. People will be called upon to re-examine themselves and may well be challenged as in the parable of the speck and the plank found in Chapter 7 of Matthew's Gospel:

Pass no judgment, and you will not be judged. For as you judge others, so you will yourselves be judged, and whatever measure you deal out to others will be dealt back to you. Why do you look at the speck of sawdust in your brother's eye, with never a thought for the great plank in your own? You hypocrite! First take the plank out of your own eye, and then you will see clearly to take the speck out of your brother's.

The passage can be taken as a direct warning against judging, condemning and dismissing people with disabilities as in some way not just different but inferior to those who consider themselves 'normal'. For although a physical or mental disability may appear obvious and be conspicuous there are aspects of mainstream society which are far more disabling to the spirit, and yet are seldom recognized to be so. One only has to think of the class system, for instance, which results in many people being dismissed as inferior because of the way they speak or dress.

There is, however, another way of approaching this question and that is to see the disability not as a hurdle or an evil or a question of discrimination but as an opportunity, a blessing.

In September 1994 the Canadian theologian Dr Mary Weir was invited to give the keynote address at an international conference of people with a particular interest in ministry to and with deaf people, held at the University of Kent at Canterbury.

Dr Weir is herself profoundly deaf. Her particular interest as a theologian is liberation theology, the twentieth-century interpretation of the Gospels developed in certain Third-World countries to make sense of the poverty and inequality of those areas.

Her address made a substantial impression both on those who heard her and on me. I read her address with great interest for it pointed to so many positive ways of approaching the subject of disability. With her permission I reproduce some substantial sections from her address, titled 'Made deaf in God's image'.

She began by describing her home, an island in the northern Pacific, just a short ferry ride from Vancouver, in British Columbia.

My home overlooks the waves pounding on a rocky beach, snow-capped mountains, islands, enormous Douglas fir and the lush green of ferns. It is a place scented with roses and cedar and strawberries, a place where the eagle soars, and surely the sunsets over the water towards Asia must be the most wonderful of anywhere on earth. I come from a beautiful place, so beautiful that it is hard to take my eyes off the summer tangle of God's good creation for a single second.

I am deaf (proudly and profoundly so!), cut off from the mainland of the hearing world by an ocean of differences, sometimes misunderstanding, and often, prejudice. Yet this island, too, is beautiful—with its immense opportunities to learn of God's goodness and grace, as well as being a place where one can experience the depths of what it is to be made by God in a way that is annoying to some and beyond the imagination of others. I have been hearing-impaired since I was seven, having learned to speak and read before God's amazing gift of deafness. I learned lip-reading mostly by the seat of my pants and really did not have the community of other deaf people to learn with, nor sign language to express my feelings and thoughts in a way that might have been so much better able to convey the depths of emotion and meaning that I was experiencing. I did grow up on an island—one of being the only deaf person I knew. That was a great deprivation! Yes, I can assure you that I have known the pain of exclusion as well as the immense weariness at trying so very hard to cope in the world of the hearing without the ability to hear. It has been in my adulthood that I have come to claim my deafness as a banner over my life and a blessing which I am called to honour and use for God's greater glory. I chose and I choose to be deaf, even though this particular gift of God has not always been to my liking. Deaf is who I am and where I come from, deaf is more than not hearing—it is being a person of vision and of touch. Perhaps it is that all deaf persons need to come to choose their deafness—as calling, as gift, and as essentially good creation. Such a choosing has certainly been a touchstone in my own life.

We live in post-modern, post-Christendom, a post-western hegemoneous world. These are times of so many old things passing away and yet the enormity of so many new things still struggling to see the light of day. Especially, our times are marked in theology as well as in politics, with the emergence of the minorities. We have liberation theology which speaks from the place of the oppressed and we have nationalists on every continent who uphold the dream of independence and ethnic fulfilment. This rise of awareness in the minorities, this articulateness of a vast diversity of peoples is both our dilemma and our glory.

The rise of deaf consciousness and pride has been a significant part of this emergence of the minorities. It has been said that the deaf are 'the last minority'. Our emergence as people proud to be who we are, with the conviction that we have a valuable part to play within the world community, the awareness of our distinct culture and languages, and also the acknowledgement of barriers in our path to self-respect, economic independence, and social (and political) acceptance is a long, long time in coming. But I think that there is no turning back. To be deaf will increasingly be to be a part of a minority people struggling for the fullness of life from the margins of society. The time when deafness was predominantly understood as being rather like a disease, or deaf people being viewed and treated like children, has to be drawing to a close. The time when deafness was hid away in the closet of society and sign language only used in the privacy of homes is past. The pity that has accompanied a long tradition of paternalism surrounding the deaf is fading—hopefully it is being replaced by mutual respect. As our minority consciousness rises, so too, I believe, does the backlash and fear from the hearing world. It has been my experience that there is more prejudice (as well as more affirmation) now in regards to deafness. I would value your impressions about that. But I am fairly sure that there has been a price to pay for the maturing of the deaf communities into minority groups.

While deaf consciousness is rising, it is also true that in many ways the uniqueness of deaf culture faces undermining factors. Captioned TV, text telephones, the demise of residential schools as well as the advent of mainstreaming, videos and fax machines has brought deaf people into a larger world at the same time that it has eroded the traditional places where the deaf gathered and sign language stories were shared. At the same time as the world is opening up, largely through technology, the deaf are faced with increasing pressure to fit it, to be 'the same', to deny their unique difference. While there has never been a bigger push to be productive and useful members of larger society, these times of high unemployment and economic restraint have made it harder for the deaf and disabled people to find those special places in the economy and in society where they are able to give their gifts. And, needless to say, unemployment has a way of undermining self-esteem in work-orientated societies. Unless, of course, the world can be moved beyond the 'Protestant Ethic' and discover a spirituality that gives value to people on a more profound and inclusive level. It could just be that the deaf have a contribution to make precisely at this point of a deeper spirituality than our production-geared wavelengths have allowed all these decades.

It is essential that theology and spirituality be a part of the movement of deaf people towards self-respect and the respect of whole humanity. This is a vulnerable and wonderful time to have made the choice to be deaf. As a community of people, indeed as a spiritual community, we need now to do things for ourselves which we have not done before. Yet we need to do them in our own way. We need to be strong enough to be secure in our identity as deaf people in order that the entire human community may be benefited by our presence. Especially in times of struggle and change, faith is vital to undergirding self-esteem and self-awareness lest we become the perpetrators of the psychological violence which we have experienced. We need to be able to be prophetically self-critical when our movement toward fulfilment becomes anything less than respectful of the whole body of God's people.

Deaf people need each other and need a pride in being who they are as the good creation of a loving God. This means that we need to 'hear the Word' in our own mother languages and to be encouraged to interpret the meaning of the Word within our own context. This means that deaf people are to pass from being objects of ministry to sharing in ministry, including the doing of theology and the shaping of our communities. Video-tape has made possible translations of the Bible into signed languages. This will have profound effects on the deaf Christian community as well as on theology. It will take time, but there can be no turning back. As with every other culture when the Bible is translated into the maternal language, ministry will become that of the newly empowered people for themselves. All of this is extremely challenging to the deaf community as well as those who have traditionally worked with us. Opportunity is here for great spiritual growth for both deaf and hearing. Yet, it will not be easy.

Theology needs to be at the centre of any liberation impulse, for people need its impetus and powerful motivational undergirding as well as its reminder that every social movement, every thrust for deeper fulfilment, must find its centre and meaning in the presence and purpose of God. The deaf cannot *stand at the centre of their struggle for a more meaningful place in the world; rather God must be seen as the presence which sustains all momentum for human dignity, integrity, justice and fulfilment. How then might we articulate a theology of liberation for the community of the deaf and disabled? Such a theology needs to be the work of Christian communities as well as scholars and this will take time and discussion and praxis (the practical working out of our beliefs). This will take time and the involvement of many. Perhaps such a doing of theology might begin to happen here this week. Towards this end, I would offer a few suggestions and possibilities.*

An appropriate theology of liberation for the differently abled and physically challenged might well take its clues from the title of Sallie McFague's book The Body of God. *Here we might begin by looking at the ecology of the Christian, and human, communities. We need the theology of social ecology that Paul gave to us in I Corinthians: the body of many members and many gifts with the mutual respect of all for each; most important, with the co-ordination of all the members being enabled by the common messianic purpose and caring of the Christ, the Creator, the Spirit. McFague talks about the theology of an ecology of the natural world; we might rather dwell on a theology of God's body which focuses on the human part of the great community of God's good creation.*

Paul's description of the Church as the many-membered Body of Christ leads us into an understanding of the essential goodness of the vast diversity of humankind. We remember as well the description of Genesis where human beings are made in the image of God: not just males, certainly not just able-bodied people, but all human beings reflect God. Indeed, it has been said (rightly I think) that the image of God is a true picture of human relationship and diversity—God's image is clear when the whole human community functions to glory. Like I Corinthians' body language, Genesis gives us also a picture of people-in-co-operative-and-co-ordinative-relationship as an image of what God is like. We are made in God's image in the sense that we are made to live in relationship, in loving diversity. When one part of God's image, God's body claims to be it all, a kind of violence occurs which is very close to idolatry. All together are God's image—and this inclusiveness is one which we were created to be. Our ideas of what God is like are also stretched as we discover the immense dimensions and diversity of human uniquenesses. We can understand ourselves as created deaf in God's image while at the very same time not denying that every human person is also part and parcel of the relational image of God. Human differences are not accidents, but rather a significant part of God's very good intentions for the world. Accordingly, deafness is to be understood as created goodness, not primarily as the lack of something essential to being human.

Probably this is all very familiar to you. Yet, in our world we have lived by a rather different model for human society. For lack of a better word, let's call this other model the 'medical model'. This model rests on a theological assumption that the image of God equals the 'normal' or the 'usual' or the 'dominant'. It defines healing as making all pretty much the same; differences become deformities to be corrected or cast out of consideration. The medical model has the seemingly benevolent aim of fixing all that is 'wrong'. Deafness is seen as 'unhealthy' or 'undesirable' and great effort is spent trying to cure it or overcome it—and when all that fails, push it out beyond the boundaries of humanness. In this model, it is assumed that 'normal' people can control, can decide what is best. So, while this might produce a real drive to understand and care for 'poor deaf people', it does not really accept deafness and deaf people as good creation. It also devalues people for whom deafness is a central and unchangeable element in their existence by insisting that the goal of healing is restoring the sound, thus ignoring the rather different gifts of vision and sensitivity that are equally part of deafness.

The medical model is not without its positive points. The energy generated from within this model has made life much more liveable for many hearing-impaired people; it has given us hearing aids, and numerous devices, speech therapy, and other ways of coping in the hearing world. Often it has promoted an atmosphere of interested pity as opposed to sheer neglect. We cannot fault advocates of the medical model with a lack of caring. Yet, we must recognize that this point of departure has had the result of demeaning the differently abled, destroying their integrity as a minority group, undermining their pride in their own culture, language, and differing abilities because these are not normal by medical definitions. Where 'perfect' has been equated with 'able-bodied' or 'hearing', the deaf do become the second-rate children of a lesser god.

I would suggest that we need a paradigm shift to the way of thinking and actively believing that considers all human beings as having the possibility of perfection—each in the wholeness of their uniqueness. Perfection should not be defined as meeting the norm of prevalent culture, but rather becoming all that God creates each to be. The model that I would propose beholds God's image in a diversity of human forms within a circle of mutual respect. Deafness would no longer be seen as all shadow or negative, disease or deficiency, but rather as a very human mixture of opportunity and dilemma, giftedness and limitation. Healing would not mean making a deaf person into a hearing person, but rather an accepting and celebrating what God gives to each person and the possibility for creative interdependence within a whole community.

Implicit in what I am suggesting is the belief that deafness is essentially a part of God's very good creation. It is a gift among many other gifts to humankind. Deafness is not by nature part of the fall—but the social stigma, prejudice, exclusion, and other deaf-related suffering certainly is! I am not denying that being hearing-impaired involves one in enormous hurt and disadvantage. That should be obvious, yet it needs to be said that this pain and society's fear of differences is not a part of God's creative intentions for the world. Deafness itself is beautiful, good creation. The problem comes not in deafness, but in fallen humanity's alienation from the intentions of our loving God. Such belief liberates deaf people to be ourselves, trusting that our gifts have a vital role to play in the world.

Indeed, the community of good creation is not complete without us. Nor is the community of God's children complete without the participation of any of the so-called minorities.

Healing in the new model of theology of the body of God, might be seen as an 'opening up' of creative potential and communication of and with each person rather than an eliminating of the differences between people. The focus in such healing is not on understanding in order to control and change the deaf, but rather on accepting in order to learn from this particular gift of God and to make best use of this gift for the sake and glory of God. Healing is a profound acceptance of reality—and finding God deep within it in love. There is a similarity with mysticism here for we give up our urges to change and control in order to accept and thereby find God in our midst. Deafness is to be accepted—and loved, even if it cannot always be liked—for in so doing we are opened up to discovering the mystery of God's intentions and presence with and through us. We can begin to ask, from such a perspective, what it is that God is giving to the world through the gift of deafness and through the lives of deaf people. We can begin to share what we have been given, aware that what we are and the gifts we bring are the very goodness of a loving Creator.

How might deaf theological perspective expand contemporary ways of thinking about God? Certainly, a deaf perspective on theology would put the accent in somewhat different places, deepening and strengthening Christian tradition with a new light shed on this mystery of who our God truly is. Since the Reformation, there has been such an emphasis on words and the Word—implicitly, the spoken word conveys and almost seems to contain the Christ event.

So often the hearing impaired have felt left out of a concept of God that is so purely verbal. We might like to approach God in terms of vision and touch, image and drama. Rather than emphasising the 'thus saith the Lord' aspect of Hebrew, as well as Protestant theology, we might rather speak of a God who gives visions and dreams, who touches us and in putting our hip out of joint makes us truly God's own. A deaf Catholic priest,

Ray Fleming, has suggested that rather than conceiving of God as a great Ear-in-the-Sky ('Lord, hear our prayer...') we might do well to develop the idea of God as the all-seeing and all-knowing One who is present in ways beyond articulation and beyond intellectual understanding. I believe we need a theology of Vision, probably a theology of Touch too. Yes, and also a new respect for silence and story as the places where God becomes known—for we who are deaf know well the depth of this language. We need a renewed appreciation of visual symbolism and imagery as a language of power and impact. Also, an understanding of God as not just one who speaks (ah, speaking, always speaking is so infinitely wearying to the hearing impaired...), but as God who is Present in the intimacy of Silence and in the heart of the Journey: the God 'in whom we live and move and have our being'. God as the passionate one rather than the unmoved mover.

The prologue of John's Gospel always moves me. For in these words about the Logos, the eternal Word, the Christ who comes so near is made concrete, real, see-able, comprehensible, and yes, touchable to my deaf sensibilities. For 'the Word became Flesh and dwelt among us... and we beheld his glory...' The divine Logos, the essence of God, who is and was and ever will be, truly does become a human being. A human being, even, like me. Deaf like me, full of vision and passion and earthiness. The Word, the Christ, does become a Sign—and we are able to behold the mystery and the power of God's body amongst us and including us. The Mystery becomes a Presence full of grace and glory.

I come from an island in that ocean that we call the Pacific. A place of sky and sea, of rain forests and setting sun. I come from a place of vision and of insight: a place where the eagle soars, and sees far, far into the heart of things as they truly are. I come bringing a prayer that God may bless the gift I bear and empower the vision that we all may see and know the wonder of the body of God, in whose image we share together. May God's unfolding creation stir our hearts and empower our spirits to live and move and have our being in awe and praise, through grace, for the glory of the divine Mystery which is Love. So be it!

While certain aspects of her address were only relevant to deaf people—the debate, for instance, about the Word—most of what she had to say can be adapted for use by people with other disabilities. While she herself would be cautious in saying that disability rather than deafness is essentially part of God's good creation and it is a gift amongst many other gifts, I am sure it is possible to say just that. It would certainly be feasible to argue that disability, whatever form it may take, is not by nature part of the fall, but that the social stigma, prejudice, exclusion and suffering connected with disability certainly are.

I said earlier that the most disabling thing about disability was the poverty. Perhaps, too, it is the stigma that is attached to certain disabilities. All that is required is for a disabled person to feel that there is a stigma for that stigma to exist.

The image of God

The challenge for every Christian is to see Christ in other human beings. In the Gospels Christ deliberately chose people in prison and those who were naked as embodiments of himself. They were people in society to whom the greatest stigma was attached. So the challenge can be transferred to disabled people; even the most severely disabled person who seems to have no interaction with the world can be seen as an embodiment of Jesus.

It is sobering to reflect on how quickly a fit, able person confident and of high self-esteem can become the dribbling and uncommunicative 'cabbage' that is looked down upon or pitied by the rest of society. It takes one second of bad driving or a blood clot in the brain causing a stroke, and then transformation is immediate.

But as people who have lived through such an experience know, the inner person does not change. They may find it impossible to speak, to form words, to move, to eat without help and yet inside they know they are who they are and who they were before the life-changing event. Who knows what is going on inside the person who has been born to a profoundly disabled life?

I remember getting just a glimpse of what was going on in the mind of one particular profoundly disabled person some nine years ago in the course of making a television programme about Jim Smith. The programme was called 'The Loneliest Man in the World' and with good reason, for Jim Smith was both blind and deaf and had lived in a residential home for twenty years in almost complete isolation. He was befriended by a Red Cross volunteer, a dedicated and patient woman called Frieda Gumn. When she first met him he had just finished two decades of life without any human contact bar the occasional touch on the shoulder or arm to tell him that a meal was ready. He could not speak, as he had never learned to when young, and it was assumed by the authorities that he was mentally handicapped.

Frieda, however, was sure that Jim was intelligent, and began the long process of introducing him to the outside world. She taught him hand sign language and various crafts. Instead of spending all his days just obsessively winding and re-winding a piece of string he learnt to plant seeds and make bags.

The most remarkable sequence in the whole film was when Jim was taken into Frieda's local parish church and allowed, through touch and smell, to experience a place of worship. His behaviour showed an unexpected reverence for the place and when he was offered the chance to take Communion hidden memories, or perhaps spiritual instinct, came to the fore.

Some people might argue that language is essential for a person to develop that unique capacity which goes with being a human. Jim Smith did not have language. Even his hand sign vocabulary was limited to two hundred words. Yet in his behaviour, dignity and demeanour he expressed a gentle and caring nature which had for over twenty years been totally ignored.

I wonder what reply we would give if Jesus asked us at the final judgment, 'Where were you when I was profoundly disabled, sitting in a wheelchair dribbling and grunting?' I hope we would all be able to answer, 'I was alongside you, so aware of your presence that I was unaware of the disability.'

8

A RE-EVALUATION

Our Western society's perceptions of disability can be traced back through the Christian heritage to New Testament times. Some of those perceptions have undoubtedly been damaging to disabled people, but the Bible stories concerning disability can be read in many different ways. Passages from the Gospels, for instance, have many layers of meaning and indeed reinterpretations and retellings of Jesus' parables can produce new insights.

A high proportion of the bit-part players in the Gospels are men and women with disabilities. It says much about the age in which, before modern medicine, life was often hard, brutish and short, but it also says much about the priorities of Jesus in placing the healing of the sick high on his agenda.

In the Middle East two thousand years ago the balance of disabilities would have been very different, which would have affected people's attitudes towards the issue. There would have been far fewer people around whose disabilities would have stemmed from birth. Many children born with disabilities would not have survived as they do today. Similarly as life expectancy was shorter there would have been fewer old people in the community enduring the disabilities of an ageing body. A far higher proportion of disabilities would have been borne by adults in middle life as a consequence of accidents which had been badly treated or illnesses and conditions far less common today. There would also have been wounds from military service and, indeed, in subsequent centuries the disabilities of returning soldiers were often the most evident.

The reports from the Gospels do much to reinforce the medical rather than the social model of disability, but the distinction did not apply two thousand years ago in the same way as it does today. Little of the technology of accessibility was available, and often the disabilities themselves were caused by medical problems and endemic disease. It is the way in which the accounts of the healing miracles are now read which reinforces that medical/social dichotomy which many disabled people are now beginning to question.

Although the physical environment of the time made it very difficult for people with mobility problems to move around freely and independently, there was little at the time that could be done about the problem. Ramps and widened doors are only relevant when disabled people have access to wheelchairs, which clearly two thousand years ago they did not. Similarly Braille or embossed public instructions were out of the question in the days before general literacy.

In the Gospels thirty-five specific miracles are described. There are three cases in which the dead are raised: Lazarus at Bethany, the widow's son at Nain and Jairus' daughter. There are also nine miracles described in which the laws of physics appear to be broken or under Jesus' unique control. These include turning water into wine, walking on water, feeding the five thousand and calming the storm. However, that leaves twenty-three miracles involving healing. Of these six refer to mental illness or demonic possession and seventeen refer to physical problems. The latter include blindness, paralysis, a withered hand and leprosy.

Mental illness or demons?

An examination of all of these cases of healing reveals the attitudes of the Gospel writers to the conditions themselves. For example, the Gospel writers and their first readers would have assumed that psychiatric problems were caused by demonic possession. This is confirmed in the other stories, some of them very graphically told. Chapter 8 of Luke's Gospel tells this story of Jesus landing with the disciples at a village on the banks of the Sea of Galilee.

*As Jesus stepped ashore he was met by a man from the town
who was possessed by devils. For a long time he had neither
worn clothes nor lived in a house, but stayed among the tombs.
When he saw Jesus he cried out, and fell at his feet shouting,
'What do you want with me, Jesus, son of the Most High God? I
implore you, do not torment me.'*

*For Jesus was already ordering the unclean spirit to come out
of the man. Many a time it had seized him, and then, for
safety's sake, they would secure him with chains and fetters;
but each time he broke loose, and with the devil in charge made
off to the solitary places.*

*Jesus asked him, 'What is your name?' 'Legion,' he replied.
This was because so many devils had taken possession of him.
And they begged him not to banish them to the Abyss.*

*There happened to be a large herd of pigs nearby, feeding on
the hill; and the spirits begged him to let them go into these
pigs. He gave them leave; the devils came out of the man and
went into the pigs, and the herd rushed over the edge into the
lake and were drowned.*

While some Christians today would accept the relevance of
demonic possession to the diagnosis of some psychiatric disorders,
most would more readily accept the other current theories involving
brain chemistry, personality disorder and upbringing. However today
for a person with a psychiatric disorder, it might be possible for him or
her to conclude from an isolated reading of the Gospel accounts that
all their mental problems were rooted in demonology.

This is not the place to develop the debate about the question of
demon possession. But any individual's reaction to and contact with a
person with a psychiatric disorder will be coloured by their own
understanding of the cause. Those with little understanding of
psychiatric disabilities are generally afraid of people behaving in strange
ways. The erroneous assumption is often made that people acting
irrationally or in an antisocial manner can be unpredictably or more
frequently violent. Fear of such people is increased if it is also believed
that peculiar and irrational behaviour is caused by malevolent and evil
supernatural beings who have hijacked a victim's reason. Thus, if one is

examining the manner in which the Christian heritage has formed the modern Western perception of disability, it is relevant to know about the belief in demon possession.

As mental illness and mental handicap are often confused, fear of the first group spills over into fear of the second and from that fear develops prejudice. Analyzing that prejudice often reveals a curious set of attitudes: people fear that those with either mental illness or learning difficulties will act in an antisocial or immoral manner. For example, local people protesting against a residential home for people with mental handicaps being set up in the neighbourhood may assume that residents will behave in an unacceptable manner and, to quote David Potter in his book *Mental Handicap*, local people may fear that children will be at risk 'because of the assumed lack of sexual restraint alleged to be common to people with mental handicaps... such objections relate to folk law rather than facts'.

Physical disability: judgment on sin?

Such attitudes are not invoked when examining the physical healings of Jesus. However, his words can be used to reinforce the attitude that disabilities are a consequence of sin.

In the Gospel of Matthew, Chapter 8, the story is told of how a paralyzed man was brought on his bed to Jesus. Jesus said to the man 'Take heart, my son, your sins are forgiven.' Then to counter the charge that to forgive sins was a blasphemy he said, 'Is it easier to say, "Your sins are forgiven", or to say, "Stand up and walk"?' Jesus then addressed his remarks directly to the paralyzed man and told him to stand up, take up his bed and then go home, at which point the man did indeed rise and walk.

However, this was not his general approach. In other descriptions of healing miracles, such as that to be found in Matthew Chapter 15, no link between sin and disability or illness is made. It seems therefore that only in very specific cases did Jesus identify a condition, possibly a cataleptic one, in which a disability was linked to a sense of guilt. Moreover, in Chapter 9 of John's Gospel, Jesus specifically refutes the general link between disability and sin:

As he walked along, he saw a man blind from birth. His disciples asked him, 'Rabbi, who sinned, this man or his parents, that he was born blind?' Jesus answered, 'Neither this man nor his parents sinned; he was born blind so that God's works might be revealed in him.'

Of course, in certain cases it can be argued that disabilities are the results of sin, or at least the error or folly of the disabled person. An obvious example would be the joyrider who steals a car, smashes it and as a result shatters his own spine, leaving him tetraplegic. But why would one young tearaway be singled out for punishment while hundreds get away with a police warning, a fine or, at most, a spell in prison? And if the punishment is supposed to be from God, can any Christian seriously argue that a lifetime's paralysis is the appropriate punishment for stealing a car?

There is a minority view of disability which incorporates an understanding of evil without pinning any blame on the disabled individual. Valerie Lang is an active member of her local church, a graduate of the London School of Economics and holds a senior research position with the Civil Aviation Authority. She has cerebral palsy, which is severe enough for her parents once to have been advised that it was best that she be put away in a home and that they forget about her. This her parents refused to do and Valerie has been able to achieve much in life. Nevertheless she has always viewed and continues to view her disability as an enormous frustration. She sees no good in being continually held back and slowed down when her mind is so full of energy.

I cannot understand therefore how a loving God would deliberately condone a disability being given to a child at birth. This is the theological problem I have wrestled with all my life. The view I have come to I know is not mainstream but I have concluded that the disability itself stems from a source of evil. That is not to say that I or any other disabled person am guilty of this evil any more than anyone else, but it is to say that the disability is not a gift of God and must therefore be the opposite. Clearly there are some instances when a disability can be attributed to human error, negligence or wickedness. But in my case it would be hard to do this and conclude that my life-long disability is in any way a just or proportionate response to something which might have been done wrong or erroneously by someone else in the past.

Disabled people as outcasts

Many disabled people talk about being isolated by their disabilities. In some instances this simply means not being able to get out and about, being institutionalized or imprisoned in their own home. However for many this isolation can exist even when the individual does have access to mainstream society. In an obvious case a person who is profoundly deaf is isolated and can therefore feel left out of the society of which they are a member. But in many other cases that sense of isolation turns into a feeling of being an outcast. Disabled people talk of feeling conspicuously different and therefore being treated as different as they go about their daily lives. This different treatment does not necessarily involve overt hostility. It is a question of body language. Wheelchair users describe how people approach them in discomfort or with diffidence, treating them not as that individual person but as one of a category. Sometimes the disabled person is made to feel different because they are approached with exaggerated concern or are offensively patronized.

One BBC researcher in his twenties, who is also a wheelchair user, recalls waiting at a supermarket check-out with his shopping and being approached by an elderly woman who patted him on the head and gave him a packet of sweets. He was lost for words but if he had reacted angrily the woman would not have understood and would have felt herself insulted.

Many Western liberals find it hard to cope with the collective guilt of being a member of an exploitative society. They not only overreact in their liberalism to compensate, but then feel affronted when their concern is challenged. This has certainly been felt in parts of the United States, where the white liberal supporters of civil rights are now as derided by the black power leaders as are the conservatives and rednecks. To many people concerned with the politics of disability, this is not an unreasonable parallel.

But to earth this debate, a simple poem by Janice Pink from the anthology of writings by disabled women *Mustn't Grumble*, makes the point:

I was waiting at the check-out and leaning on my crutch
When a voice behind me loudly said, 'Come, come this is too much!

'Hey Miss,' she called. 'Young lady! I say! Now listen, dear,
You'd better get a move on, we've got a cripple here!'

The cashier's tapping fingers stopped, she looked around to see
Who this pathetic creature was—I realized it was me...

'Now let me help unpack your load—the least that I can do—
Because, but for the grace of God, I could be just like you!

'Does anybody help you? Or do you live alone?
Oh, do you buy this in a tin? I always bake my own.

'You haven't got a husband? Well build a social life—
Perhaps you'll meet a crippled man who wants a crippled wife!'

I found this quite offensive, and told her so, at length,
She said, 'My dear, I understand—you've lost your health and
  strength.

'I know you're being very brave, but that was rather rude—
Next time someone helps you, try to show some gratitude.

'Of course you think life isn't fair, but when you're feeling blue—
Big smile! And then remember, there's someone worse than you!'

It is perhaps not too far-fetched to include references to the radical wing of the disability lobby in the context of examining the Christian attitude to disability, for it is frequently argued that Jesus himself was a social radical, as his story of the Good Samaritan shows: the Samaritan, the despised outsider, is the one person who will help someone in trouble.

In the Spring 1993 edition of the publication *All People*, produced by Church Action on Disability, there appears this account, written by

Faith Bowers, of a play which takes the story out of its original cultural context without destroying its essential meaning.

A man had an epileptic fit in the high street. He writhed around on the ground, his shopping rolling out of his bag. Eventually he lay still and unconscious.

Two women came along, also out shopping. One was in a wheelchair, which her friend pushed. They looked at the prostrate man and wondered whether they ought to do something, but a glance at a watch suggested they could not afford the delay so they hurried on.

A priest came along, his nose deep in his prayer book. He walked past the man without apparently noticing him at all.

In reeled a drunken old tramp. As he lurched along, he stumbled over the obstruction, and it dawned on him that something was not right. He tottered back and had a good look. He was concerned. Clumsily he began to gather the scattered shopping back into the bag and set it at the side of the pavement. Then he went back to the poor man, who was just beginning to stir. The tramp knelt beside him, produced the most dreadful filthy handkerchief and tenderly, tenderly mopped the man's mouth.

As he revived, the tramp assisted him and guided him to a seat. With a plastic bag as a make-shift bandage he bound the man's forehead. From his pocket, he took his precious bottle, pulled the stopper with his teeth, and gave the poor man a reviving swig. Finally he sat down beside the man and held him in his arms until he recovered.

This modern interpretation of the Good Samaritan was devised and acted by a group of people with severe learning disabilities. The tramp, so hilarious in his dreadfulness, so Christ-like in his compassion, bore the familiar features of Down's Syndrome.

A group of friends live in a Shaftesbury Society home and worship at Harlow Baptist Church. They have found among them real acting talent and are using this gift to make the Gospel known to others.

At Easter many of their friends from their day centre and elsewhere around the town came to the church to see them re-enact the passion story. On that occasion Philip had played Jesus, the play culminating as he hung motionless in the spotlight on the cross. He grinned as he told me he had been brought back to earth with a bump when given the role of a filthy tramp. His friend Robert, who played the priest, is the group's wardrobe master. He has discovered a talent for improvising costumes from the group's limited resources.

Many people who learn to speak late develop useful communication skills in mime and can also apply this to dramatic effect. It is exciting when that skill in turn is harnessed for Christian witness.

For me, that mime went way beyond sympathetic interest in the activities of people with such disabilities. It was by any standards a powerful religious experience. For me the good Samaritan will long remain a dirty old tramp with Down's features.

In the case of the healing of lepers Jesus was specifically seen to help individuals whose disabilities had made them outcasts. The message which can be read from these stories is that Jesus was prepared to confront the social attitudes which had resulted in such people being placed beyond the pale. Lepers were quite literally untouchable and so in one account found in Luke's Gospel, a special point is made of Jesus touching the leper to cure him. The leper had approached Jesus and begged him for help: 'If only you will, you can cleanse me.' Luke says Jesus stretched out his hand, touched him and the leprosy left him immediately.

A superficial reading of the passage would suggest a straightforward account of a healing; the depth to the passage comes when it is realized how the social attitudes of the day were being radically challenged by Jesus being prepared to touch a leper.

These days groups of people may still be seen walking together, causing others in mainstream society to keep their distance, a little frightened and embarrassed—a party of adults with severe learning difficulties out and about shopping or going on a visit. Not long ago a group of such people stirred controversy in a Devon seaside resort. When they arrived on holiday the local townsfolk felt that their appearance and manners were so off-putting that others would not want to come to their town to spend their money and enjoy their holidays. An unlikely comparison one might suppose—parties of docile adults with learning difficulties and gangs of contagious lepers. But is the comparison so unreasonable? The fear of catching leprosy from contact with the lepers was a far more powerful influence on society than the reality. A single contact with a leper was unlikely to prove fatal. The fear of touching the lepers was similar to the fear of touching Aids patients. Indeed, the term 'leper' is now most commonly used as a synonym for the outcast. Similarly, the fear people have of those with learning difficulties is far more powerful than any real chance that they might do harm or act violently. It is just that the sight of people who are different and normally kept out of sight by society stirs deep-seated fears in the subconscious.

In understanding disability from a Christian perspective, the Gospel accounts of Jesus' ministry must be understood at a more than superficial level. Jean Vanier writes in *Be Not Afraid*:

Jesus manifests himself as He walks through Judea, when He comes to give sight to the blind, to enable the lame man to walk and the deaf to hear. And these are essentially symbols of something much deeper. He opens the eyes of the heart, so that we begin to see reality as it is, so that we see our wounded brothers, see their anguish. He opens our ears, for just as we see but are blind to reality, so we hear but do not listen. There is a fundamental healing that must take place before we really can listen to the music of reality, before we can listen to people without fear, before we can listen to the Spirit.

Jesus the Healer comes when we are conscious that we need a healer; when we become conscious of our own egoism, all the anarchy of desire, all the fears, all the cowardice and weakness, all the need for human security that incites us to possess. It is only when we become conscious of our weakness and our fears that we can begin to grow in union with the Spirit.

Thus while a surface reading of the Gospel stories might suggest they are simply tales of a Palestinian do-gooder with an effective healing touch, and a *mis*reading of the Gospel stories might suggest they are simply about a relationship between physical imperfection and sin, perhaps the true reading of the stories is a challenge to every reader to face up to and be healed of their own inner fears.

Any answers?

It is frequently the case that to come to a Christian understanding of the nature and purpose of disability one cannot go to a specific biblical passage for instant answers. Much has to be teased out of the texts; there will be many texts that will be relevant to the whole understanding and then, as is so often the case in understanding the Bible, the evidence has to be transposed to another place and another time. And although there are many references to disabled people, the paralyzed, the palsied, those with dropsy, indeed in the language of the Authorised Version those with 'divers diseases and torment' the Bible has no direct answers to the question— *why* have these things happened to these people?

In the parallel tradition of Islam a disability or illness is accepted simply as the will of Allah. In twentieth-century Western culture, when a child is born with a disability the parents ask the doctor why. They are given the immediate cause, maybe a difficult birth or a genetic abnormality. However, the deeper questions, 'Why me?' 'Why us?' are much harder to answer, and the medical profession has no response.

Does the Christian church have answers to offer? Can it explain the purpose of disability; that is, if there is a purpose and disability is not just a random occurrence? It is very easy for those who do not pin their understanding of life on faith in a just and merciful God, to point to the random nature of disability and say it is just bad luck, a chance happening. In scientific terms they might refer to a genetic disorder and say that it is evidence of natural selection at work. From time to time, it might be argued, genetic changes have to be thrown up by the chaos of creation in order that improvements to the species can evolve. If genetic change is a random process then defects will occur as well as improvements, and organisms with these defects will simply die off.

There is danger in thinking like this; the implication is that by the laws of the jungle the weak are disposable and the strong survive. In a purposeless universe the wasted mutations of random selection are discarded; in such an understanding there is no room for morality, for the argument that all human life is special, and that those who appear to be outside the parameters of physical or mental normality should be given every opportunity to thrive and grow. Such an approach can lead to the gas chambers.

Yet it is equally dangerous and unsatisfactory for pastors and clergy to shrug their shoulders and say it is all a mystery, or to take the approach described earlier in Chapter 5 by one disabled woman from Ireland, interviewed on the Radio Four 'Does He Take Sugar?' programme. She told how, at the convent where she was educated, the nuns would talk patronizingly of God's 'special people' and 'little angels', while others in her community would talk darkly about the sins of the families returning in the form of disability.

Some theologians have constructed elaborate and apparently plausible explanations. One such, who appeared on 'Does He Take Sugar?' in June 1992, told a moving story of how his own intellectual approach was shaken to the roots by an encounter with a disabled baby. The baby was called Alex and his brief life forced the theologian, Dr David Pailin, to reassess his key ideas. In a book he called *A Gentle Touch* Dr Pailin wrote movingly about his brief encounter with the little child who was to have such a profound effect on his thinking.

I met him when his mother brought him down on occasions to the chaplaincy. I once helped feed him and he blew bubbles and covered my spectacles with hard setting baby food. I held him, I smiled at him, we shook hands when he learnt that particular skill, and I was interested in him because his parents were friends.

What I learnt, as I thought about it, was that the problem that I thought Alex posed because of handicap was in fact the problem of the significance of human being as such. That it was wrong to isolate the handicapped as if they were some separate species within humanity, and I began to realize that in fact what the handicapped do is point all of us to our finitude and the question, what is the worth of a human being? Because we all start in a profoundly handicapped state, new born infants of all parents are very limited in what they can do beyond shouting for food and many of us will finish in a very handicapped state. For many people there are very limited possibilities anyway for creative action throughout their life, because of the economic and social situations in which they found themselves, so I began to realize that theology had very often been talking about the significance of the human in terms of middle-class, rather able people with considerable resources at their disposal, the kind of middle-class people of the first world, and that was a profound mistake, and therefore I had to go back and say, well what is the significance of the human?

I think the significance of the human, the worth of the human does not lie in anything that is achieved, I think we've got into a mind set where we think that value is something that we gain by what we produce. I remember going into a café and finding there a person who was very limited in her abilities, she'd been taken in by a couple of young friends, and as they went out somebody saying, 'Well, what can she contribute to society?' And this worried me enormously and there are many cases like this and I began to realize that the value of the human does not lie in what we achieve but in what we are of worth to others, in other words value is given and it is given by the love, the care, the concern of others, and supremely I began to realize by the love of God for each individual. It's not what we offer to God that is important, but what God offers to us.

So Dr Pailin had gone back to the old Protestant ideas of the Reformation, salvation through grace rather than works. Where did he think the church had gone wrong in its teaching since?

I think it's been taken over by the Protestant ethics, so-called, of achievement, of doing things, of achieving things, I think that we've also begun to pick this up from the materialistic society in which we find ourselves, as people who benefit from the material gains that have gone on since the Enlightenment in the world in which we find ourselves.

It is a great mistake to think that we must try and impose our values onto others. We must allow people, whatever their situation, to be themselves, and I think we impose great demands on young people particularly, as parents, as teachers, as colleagues, when we try to get them to conform to our image of what is the good life. And people must be allowed to develop their own individual characteristics according to their interest and their abilities.

Dr Pailin was speaking at a time when the case of a little girl, Laura, being taken to America for a series of multiple, frontier operations, was much in the news. Everyone admired her brave demeanour and hundreds of thousands of pounds were given to enable her to have the very latest treatment. Sadly, she died. What would Dr Pailin say from his new position to the parents of such a child doing their best both to save a life and to right that which seemed to be abnormal?

I can well understand the great concern of a parent to do everything that they can for their child, I think in allowing a child to be themselves we must give them every opportunity to be such, on the other hand I think there is also a very hard question that society has to raise, namely how far can we support individuals? We could put enormous funds into the medical and social care services in order to make the quality of life better for certain people, but we have to ask the question, at what point does this in fact begin to create a deterioration in the quality of life generally because the demands are too great? And I think it's a very hard question and one that too often we shy from, we do not ask, now then: what is the proper responsibility of society, in facing the fact that some people in fact do die young?

But what about the person who is born with a profound disability? Could it be seen by some, particularly by the parents in that time of adjustment, sometimes of anger, that this is one of God's mistakes? If they blamed God, what would Dr Pailin say to them?

I think it is a very understandable reaction. On the other hand when one thinks about it the doctrine of creation, it cannot credibly be understood to hold that God is responsible for everything that happens. We have to think about the doctrine of creation in terms of what the scientists tell us about the development of the cosmos, about biological evolution, about the development of the DNA chains and so on, and the fact that a child is born handicapped means that something has gone wrong in a process that normally performs in a way that does not lead to that situation. Something has happened within a DNA chain, maybe and a handicap has developed, a virus has affected it maybe, and that is one of those situations that happen in order that there be a certain amount of freedom within the world. So that there can be development, there must also be the risk of things going wrong as well as improvements occurring. And I think the basic question comes back to, what do we mean by the notion of God as creator? I don't believe that any longer we can hold that God is in charge of everything, designing a virus, designing a DNA chain, and then implementing it and therefore being totally responsible for what happens. I think the creator is much more to be seen as one who leaves the autonomy to the created order to develop itself according to its own system of chance and necessity.

Yet one of the messages which surely comes from the Gospel accounts of the healing miracles is that God can intervene and appear to overturn the created order?

I think if God has the ability to intervene and does not, then God is morally responsible in a way that to me would cease to allow God to be an object of worship. A person who sees that something disastrous is going to happen and has the power to intervene and does not use it, seems to me to be somebody that is morally reprehensible, whether it be a parent or God.

Thus Dr Pailin challenges a whole area of Christian ministry in which healers claim to be used as channels through which God performs miracles today. Yet he also makes the very profound point that everyone, including disabled people, if valued as individuals and accepted as created in the image of God, come by their essential selves and personalities in some way other than by their outward appearance or material structure.

In struggling for a Christian understanding of God's purpose in allowing disability, there are no simple explanations. As there are so many immediate causes of disability, indeed every disabled individual has a unique history, perhaps there is no single overarching theory. One certainly cannot take the Gospel stories at face value to construct a theory. They are many-layered. Through reading and contemplation, an individual pondering his or her own circumstances may find personal guidance, but is unlikely to be able to construct an overall theory.

However, if it does show one thing, an exploration of the world of disability from a Christian background should indicate that it is through misreading the Gospels that prejudice and fear arises. For to be afraid of or prejudiced against someone for their physical or mental disabilities is to make the basic error that all that exists of that person exists in a material form.

If everyone is created in the image of God, it is patently obvious that that image is not a material one—everyone is physically and mentally different. That quality which mirrors the Creator is not reliant upon the shape of the body or the clarity of the mind. So Christians should not categorize and react to any individual according to their disability, but see beyond the superficial to the deeper and essential person. Even if an individual appears to have no hearing, sight, speech or communication, that person, being born of human parents, nevertheless retains all human dignity.

Similarly, the disabled person who feels a hatred of their body and a self-loathing can remind themselves that their real self is not that figure they see in the mirror. Of course, this is easy to say. For the individual shattered by a trauma or disfigurement, it appears that the whole world has collapsed. Often in despair people turn to drugs and drink, turn in on themselves, feel unloved and reject all love, or even attempt suicide. Much of this will be because of their own fears of disability. It is in that context that the reaction of friends, with or without a faith, is crucial. Frequently other people's reactions compound the problems;

inappropriate advice is given with the best intentions, and always there is a sense that there is a barrier between the newly disabled person and the rest of the world.

The Cornish poet Jack Clemo had personal experience of this great barrier between a disabled person and the rest of the world, for Jack Clemo was both blind and deaf. He resolved the conundrum of disability in a harsh and stark manner which made much sense to him but which many would find impossible to empathize with or emulate.

His poetry concentrated not on the beauties of creation but on the grit and pain of the human battle with the earth for ownership of its resources. He wrote of the machinery of the Cornish clay works, and how God was to be found in the stark landscape of the disembowelled Cornish soil. And he saw God's plan when he wrestled with the question, why had he been singled out to endure a dual disability? He found the answer in Calvinism, that strict and unyielding product of the Protestant Reformation which asserts that only certain chosen people are God's elect and they must first have to undergo the tests and trials of this world.

If the purpose of this world is to be the proving ground other questions follow. Why are some people given tougher tests than others? The Gospel logic can suggest that those who have it easy here on earth will find it harder to enter the Kingdom of Heaven. The story of what happens to the rich Dives and the poor Lazarus after death illustrates this point, as does the saying that it is easier for a camel to go though the eye of a needle than for a rich man to enter the Kingdom of Heaven. However, as with all clues from the Bible, none can be taken in isolation and used accordingly. Such thinking may have brought comfort to many impoverished people in the past, but it has also been used cynically by the better-off to maintain their own positions of privilege. Slave owners two centuries ago argued that their slaves were more blessed because of their subjugation to their masters and the earthly indignities they tolerated.

Similarly, translating from the terms of slavery to those of disability, there are many dangers in talking of disabled people as being specially blessed. It can quickly become the sentimental talk, referred to earlier, sometimes used by members of religious communities and others looking after disabled children, when they refer to them as being 'so sweet as to be God's little angels'.

It would be wrong to condemn those who adopt such an approach. It is one way, consistent to them and their beliefs, of making sense of the work they do, and many people, particularly some in religious communities, who have worked in isolation for so long would be deeply hurt by the remarks of those who are now politically active in the disability movement in thinking that their work is despised. Much of that work is sheer drudgery; it involves wiping dribbling mouths, washing doubly incontinent teenagers and patiently feeding people who appear to have no comprehension of the world. Unless these people are idealized the work may seem pointless, and if much of the cultural imagery involves the sentimentality of popular Catholicism, that is the form the idealism will take. It is certainly an approach consistent with Christ's message that we should all see him in the very least in society.

But to return to the theological examination of disability: some people who find their disability extremely frustrating interpret their lives as a battle against evil. As with Valerie Lang, they do not say that the disability was caused by an evil deed in the past or that it is in any sense a punishment but that, for whatever reason, the disability itself is not good—and the opposite of good is evil.

The frustration of disability is thus seen as a test. Is it, though, a test placed there by God? Not if one believes in a good God, although it might make sense if one believes that both good and evil exist in the one God, or that both good and evil are the creations of the Almighty.

Are disabilities God's mistakes? Or do they occur as part of God's order, a literal manifestation of what the Bible means when it says that the sins of the parents can be visited upon subsequent generations? After all, certain conditions are transmitted genetically. On the other hand, perhaps disabilities are created quite deliberately by a loving creator in order to stimulate us.

That would be a very unsettling notion to entertain. Yet there are many cases of disabled children who have had a profound effect on the families into which they were born and who have stimulated immense acts of devotion and love. But this stretches an understanding of God's purpose to an extreme which few would readily entertain.

My own approach

How do I make sense of the confusion of ideas and ethics thrown up by disability?

Firstly, by accepting that everybody is created in the image of God and, as Dr Pailin discovered, even the tiniest and most profoundly disabled children can speak to us of their Creator.

Secondly, I would suggest that the evil associated with disability should not be used to produce stereotype characterizations but should be understood for what it really is. Disability is not the work of the devil, although sometimes it is caused by human folly, weakness or sin, but may frequently be associated with evil, those negative reactions which it can trigger in others. The consequent stigmatization or prejudice is very real. And that evil, I would suggest, is a product of fear. So many myths and misunderstandings exist about disability that people are fearful of it, and disabled people have been kept out of sight and out of mind for so long people do not know how to respond to them.

Everyone is in some way fearful of disability. No able-bodied person likes to think of the possibility of losing their mobility, even though it is accepted by all that disability can strike at any time. However, we all accept risk in our lives. We know risks are involved in driving a motor vehicle, travelling on a train, going up a step ladder, changing a light bulb, cooking, boiling a kettle, the list is endless. It would be impossible to live any meaningful life if one insisted on eradicating risk. So we all live with that tension.

Disabled people have to take similar decisions, and some are much closer to the frontier between life and death. Someone requiring mechanical assistance with breathing knows that travelling in any form is hazardous. Someone with cerebral palsy knows that such day-to-day domestic tasks as making a cup of tea are fraught with danger. And in the same way that all human beings take risks, even though they fear the possible but unlikely consequences, so all disabled people have to live with the fear of disability. They may be in control and unafraid of their *own* disability, but any other form is foreign territory. A wheelchair user is fearful of going blind in the same way as any other person, while a blind person, living in a sightless world, would fear incontinence, loss of speech, or having to rely on a wheelchair.

I can recall from my own experience how, for the years leading up to kidney dialysis, I was fearful of the whole process. I wanted to deny that this would be my destiny. I would see people with tubes carrying blood from their arms through a machine and back into their bodies again. They would be lying there for hour upon hour, seemingly submissive to the medical system. I hated the idea that I, too, would be one of them. And yet within a few months of starting regular dialysis, I had found my way of coping. I knew there were risks involved in dialysing and at least once had a close shave when an air bubble got into my line. But once I was used to the procedures I did not fear them. Once I was in control it was no longer my ogre. My fears of dialysis were replaced by other fears. What if I should get diabetes? What if I should have a stroke and be unable to communicate my thoughts?

So one aspect of disability, whether we are able-bodied or disabled, is that there is always a disability we dread. It is largely the fear of the unknown heightened by images and nightmares we have locked away inside us; nevertheless, that dread is real. If it can be argued that prejudice and embarrassment are natural consequences of fear, then they are natural reactions to disability.

Having said, however, that they are natural, that is not to say such reactions are good. What religion teaches, or at least should teach, especially Christianity, are ways—such as trust and mutual respect—by which each individual can address and cope with his or her fears. In my view, this is the role of theology in the disability debate. It is a more fundamental role than that rather superficial political view where issues have to be seen in black and white terms as matters of rights.

The secular civil rights approach to disability deals largely with prejudice and injustice enountered by disabled people; but these are symptoms. Unlike theology it is not equipped to tackle the root problem: fear. Controlling symptoms is very necessary and, in terms of the comprehensive civil rights legislation proposed by private members in Parliament, essential. It is necessary to outlaw the sort of discrimination against people in the workplace and in public life which only increases prejudice. If a person never meets a disabled colleague at work, because it is the policy of the firm never to employ someone with a disability, then that person will have no opportunity to overcome his or her fears through personal contact and friendship. But it takes a deeper approach to exorcise the fear inside all of us.

Yet in the context of Christian teaching, which is quite ready to address many other aspects of fear and to talk of trust in God, tackling the ingrained and natural fear of disability is not easy. First of all Christians must re-examine how they and their forebears have been responsible for creating much of this fear. There is a need to move away from viewing disabled people as objects of pity and people who especially need the mercy and grace of God.

To counter some of the negative images of disabled people in the Bible, positive role models who are disabled need to be found; people of deep spirituality who are known to have a disability, but whose disabilities are only incidental to their full and purposeful lives.

Furthermore, to meet and overcome the fear of disability there is the need for theologians and other thinkers in society to stress the positive aspects of life with disability. Everybody in life has some form of disability, whether it attracts that label or not, and every life consists of a rich mix of fulfilment and disappointment, opportunity and discouragement.

Strange as it may seem, when I look back on my own kidney problems, I know that the whole package of experience was enriching and enabling to me. And, time after time, I have heard disabled people say to me that they are who they are not in spite of but including the disability. It has shaped their character, often for the better, making them more determined, more compassionate or more sociable. Mary Weir's contribution in the last chapter, in which she talked about herself being created in the image of God and seeing her disability as a blessing, fits into this pattern. Because of her deafness she believes her other senses have a heightened awareness and she is more especially tuned in to the mood and emotions of others.

One of the hardest areas to think through involves charity. Disabled people rely on others and often, through their helplessness in certain circumstances, bring out the best in others. It is not however always easy to be on the receiving end of good intentions and, indeed, this can be a corrupting force on both parties in the relationship.

Here both the giver and the receiver of help need to discover a humility which is very difficult to acquire. The giver of help needs to do so without expecting reward, or even that glow of self-satisfaction many enjoy. There needs to be a willingness on their part to learn from the disabled person they are helping, to rely on that person and take opportunities to be in their hands—maybe through seeking their advice and opinions rather than just seeing them as recipients of bonhomie and treats. Equally the disabled person needs to be attuned to the helper's subtle signs of emotion and to be willing to provide support where required and to offer friendship, even where this may be unrewarding. That support may simply be offering oneself as a listener and a friend—rare and valued qualities in both able-bodied and disabled people.

These are some of my impressions and thoughts, but my overwhelming conclusion involves the uniqueness of each individual person. In disability there should be no labelling and no assumptions, for everyone is an individual, inimitable and unrepeatable. Each of us has an obligation in life to recognize our talents over and above our disadvantages and make the fullest use of them wherever possible.

As to the question, 'Why does God allow disability to happen?', even to ask that is to query the purpose and nature of creation. We have free will and therefore have every right to seek answers but I suspect—at least in this life—we will not find any.

INDEX

A

A Gentle Touch   145
Algeria   13
All People   140
Andrews, Dr Malcolm   44–56
'Ask Us'   102, 103
Association for the Integration of Disabled
   People   34
Atlanta   98
Austin, Molly   108–110

B

Barbara, Wanda   59
Barcelona   98
Bedlam   58
Belfast   64
Be Not Afraid   100, 143
Berry, Andy   42
The Body of God   127
Bond, James (films)   30, 52
Booth, Tim & Wendy   108–110
Bowers, Faith   141–142
British Broadcasting Corporation   7, 8, 13,
   29, 139
British Council of Organisations of Disabled
   People   91
Broadcasting Research Unit   38
Brussels   86
Butler, Millie   104

C

Camera, Archbishop Helder   85
Calvinism   150
Captain Hook   52
Care in the Community   36
Causeway   101
Central Electricity Generating Board   112
Cerebral Palsy   10, 42, 63
CHAD   21, 22, 140
Children in Need   30, 36, 45
A Christmas Carol   43–44
Citizens Advice Bureaux   84
Civil Aviation Authority   138
Civil Rights Disabled Persons Bill   24, 31,
   117–121
Clemo, Jack   150
Cologne   32
Cork   90

Cotes, Ken   87
Crewe, Quentin   42
Cumberbatch, Guy   38
Cumming, Gordon   107
Customs and Excise   81–82

D

Dachau   32
Daily Telegraph   117
Darwin, Charles   11
David Copperfield   49, 54
Deginer, Teresia   88–89
Department of Health   24
Department of Social Security   83
Dessau   57
Mr Dick   44
Dickens, Charles   43–56
The Dickensian   44
Disability Alliance   44
Disability Living Allowance/Disability Working
   Allowance   82–83
Disabled Peoples International   86
Dives and Lazarus   150
Dodds, Margaret   67, 70
'Does He Take Sugar?'   7, 15, 26, 29, 32,
   43, 59, 103, 112, 114, 117, 145
Downing Street   24
Down's Syndrome   57, 98, 100, 108, 141
Dublin   87

E

East Grinstead Hospital   112
Elleker, Nick   100
European Disabled People's Parliament
   86–95
European Parliament   86

F

Fleming, Ray   131
Flynn, Paddy   87

G

Gallop, Sam   111–117
Galway   87
Genesis, book of   127
German Federation of Disabled Employers
   35
Germany   32–36, 60, 88

Gibson, Elizabeth 107
Glasgow 77, 106
Glasgow Council for Single Homeless 75
Glasgow Royal Infirmary 107
Good Samaritan 140
Guinea Pig Club 111, 112
Gumn, Frieda 133

H

Hague, William 83
Hanover 32
Harlow Baptist Church 141
Hinduism 12
Hitler 31, 33, 36
Holocaust 31
Household Words 51
Hurst, Rachel 86, 94–95, 117–21

I

Independent Living Fund 96
Islam 12, 144

J

Jairus' daughter 135
Jesus Christ 36, 79, 84, 95, 100, 132–38, 140, 142–43
John, Gospel of 131, 137
Joseph Roundtree Foundation 105
Judaism 12, 32

K

Keith, Lois 74
KeyRing 103–106
King, Martin Luther 9

L

Lang, Jimmy 77
Lang, Valerie 138–139, 151
L'Arche 100
Lawla, Rita 93
Lawton, Michael 32, 35
Lazarus 135
Leviticus, book of 85
Liverpool 41
Living with Kidney Failure 13–15
London School of Economics 138
London Zoo 78
'The Loneliest Man in the World' 133
Long John Silver 52
Long, Stuart 105
Longley, Clifford 117–121
Lourdes 79–80
Lower Saxony 33

Luke, Gospel of 142
Luther, Martin 57–58, 72

M

Mace, Sharon 93
McFague, Sallie 127
McIndoe, Sir Archibald 112
McManus, Ann & Jill 64, 68–70
Madrid 98
Mallinson, Eric 83
Master Humphrey's Clock 46
Martin, Sally 101
Marxism 12
Mason, Michelle 75
Mathers, Muriel & Sarah 65, 67, 70
Matthew, Gospel of 137
Mental Handicap... Is Anything Wrong? 57, 99, 137
Milton Keynes 36
Moby Dick 52
Morgan, Cameron 107
Munich 34
Munro, Jacqueline 76
Murphy, Margaret 106
Mustn't Grumble 74, 140

N

Nain 135
Naples 87
National Childbirth Trust 40
Nazis 31–32, 34–35, 56, 58–60
Negrine, Ralph 38
Nicholas Nickelby 52

O

The Old Curiosity Shop 46
Oliver, Professor Mike 44–56, 117–121
Olmecs 57
O'Neil, Elaine 90
Opportunities for People with Disabilities 111
Orkney 15

P

Pailin, Dr David 145–148, 152
Paralympic Games 28, 98
ParentAbility 40
Parenting Under Pressure 108–110
Partridge, James 17
Paul, apostle 85, 127
Pease, Marlene 29
Peirce, Rev. John 21
Pescud, Phil 104
Pink, Janice 140

Poland   12
Politically Correct Phrasebook   29
Poll, Carl   104–106
Potter, David   57, 99, 137
Prigent, Maria & Ashling   65
ProjectAbility   106–107
Project 12   106–107
Publishers Week   29

R
Race Relations Act   25
RADAR   10, 28, 41, 42
Red Cross   133
Rees, Nigel   29
Richard III   43
Richmond Fellowship   75
Right from the Start   62
Robertson, Nancy   21
Rudge, Barnaby   44

S
SCOPE (Spastics Society)   40, 42, 62
Scott, Sir Nicholas   117
SENSE NI   64–68
Selisara, Teresa   92
Shaftesbury Society   141
Shakespeare   43
Should the Baby Live?   34
Singer, Peter   34
Smith, Jim   133
Smith, Simon   59–61
Social Security Act 1975   82
South Africa   12, 25
Spina Bifida & Hydrocephalus   72
Staffordshire County Council   82–83
Stanton, Marion   10–11
Steady Eddy   18, 58

Steer, Alan   102
Stoke Mandeville   30
'Sunday'   8, 13

T
Telethon   30, 45, 92
Thatcherism   12
Tiny Tim Guild   56
Tolland, Frances & Marie-Louise   66–68
Tutu, Archbishop Desmond   12

U
United Kingdom   36
United States of America   11, 28, 73
University of Greenwich   44, 96, 117
University of Kent at Canterbury   44, 123
'The Useless Eaters'   59

V
Vancouver, British Columbia   123
Vanier, Jean   100, 143
Vanier, Dr Terese   100
Vietnam   73

W
Warner, Michelle   104
Weber, Frank   32
Weir, Dr Mary   20, 123–131
Whittaker, Kati   117
Williams, Peter   112
Wilson, Gordon & Marie   73
Witcher, Sally   44–56
Wood, Richard   91–92

Y
Yately   100–101